T0095864

5

The Twenty First Century

Above: The Millennium Bridge at dusk complimenting the Ha'penny Bridge in the background at high tide.

Dublin Corporation's policy of creating increased access and facilities for pedestrians lead to the renovation of the O'Connell Street area and the subsequent reduction of traffic through it in the late 1990s. This then resulted in a call for designs for a pedestrian bridge over the River Liffey, linking the Temple Bar area on the south side with the Jervis Street and Henry Street areas on the city's north side.

The new bridge would be situated 125 metres upstream from the existing pedestrian Ha'penny Bridge which is now recognised internationally as one of the iconic symbols of Dublin. The elaborate brief called for a structure that should complement and respect the existing bridge and attracted 153 Irish and international entries. The winning design team were Howley, Harrington Architects with Price & Myers as consulting engineers.

The bridge itself was designed as a lightweight steel truss which measured just over 40 metres in length and 4 metres wide and was supported at each side on granite faced, concrete abutments. Ascon Construction was appointed as the successful contractor for the project.

The bridge was fabricated by Thompson Engineering in Carlow, Co. Kilkenny and transported the 90 kilometres to Dublin as a single unit. Despite its overall weight of some 60 tons and unusual size, it was lifted and placed into position by a single crane at night to minimise traffic disruption.

260

The building programme of six months was achieved by the contractors despite the difficulty of working in such an unfavourable location. Because of the project's importance, the contractor agreed to fix the price of the tender figure and the structure was named 'The Millennium Bridge'.

The bridge fulfiled all its design requirements and received many awards due to the quality of the construction and its overall style. Awards were made by the Royal Institute of the Architects of Ireland (RIAI), the Construction Industry Federation (Ireland), the Royal Institute of British Architects (RIBA), the Institution of Structural Engineers (UK), the Emerging Architecture Award and Opus Plan Expo 2000.

Above: Manhole covers disguised with Sixties emblems allow access to the abutments located at either end of the bridge.

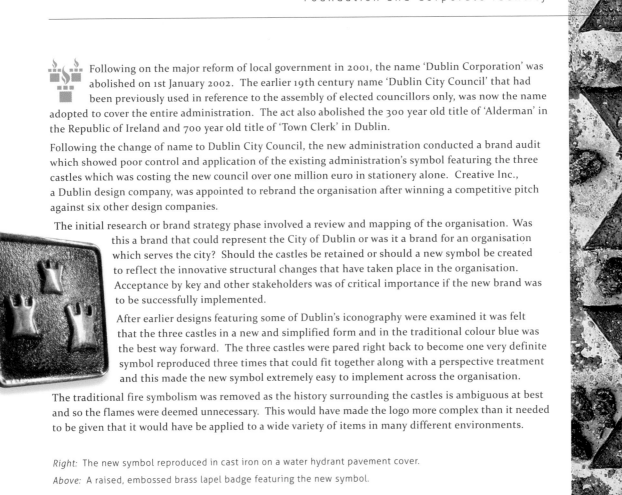

Following on the major reform of local government in 2001, the name 'Dublin Corporation' was abolished on 1st January 2002. The earlier 19th century name 'Dublin City Council' that had been previously used in reference to the assembly of elected councillors only, was now the name adopted to cover the entire administration. The act also abolished the 300 year old title of 'Alderman' in the Republic of Ireland and 700 year old title of 'Town Clerk' in Dublin.

Following the change of name to Dublin City Council, the new administration conducted a brand audit which showed poor control and application of the existing administration's symbol featuring the three castles which was costing the new council over one million euro in stationery alone. Creative Inc., a Dublin design company, was appointed to rebrand the organisation after winning a competitive pitch against six other design companies.

The initial research or brand strategy phase involved a review and mapping of the organisation. Was this a brand that could represent the City of Dublin or was it a brand for an organisation which serves the city? Should the castles be retained or should a new symbol be created to reflect the innovative structural changes that have taken place in the organisation. Acceptance by key and other stakeholders was of critical importance if the new brand was to be successfully implemented.

After earlier designs featuring some of Dublin's iconography were examined it was felt that the three castles in a new and simplified form and in the traditional colour blue was the best way forward. The three castles were pared right back to become one very definite symbol reproduced three times that could fit together along with a perspective treatment and this made the new symbol extremely easy to implement across the organisation.

The traditional fire symbolism was removed as the history surrounding the castles is ambiguous at best and so the flames were deemed unnecessary. This would have made the logo more complex than it needed to be given that it would have be applied to a wide variety of items in many different environments.

Right: The new symbol reproduced in cast iron on a water hydrant pavement cover.

Above: A raised, embossed brass lapel badge featuring the new symbol.

This extensive project included the development of brand guidelines for application across all environments including external and internal signage, press, print, stationery, the liveries of council vehicles, uniforms and usage across all digital formats. More importantly it also required buy-in from all the key stakeholders and the successful introduction of the new identity to the council's 7000 employees. This involved a programme of induction via the use of multimedia and other forms of communication.

In 2006, as part of the ongoing process of monitoring the application of the brand, Creative Inc. conducted a review of the identity guidelines and produced the updated brand guidelines manual.

263

Logo designs and Images courtesy of Creative Inc.

This page: Part of the design process which the public doesn't see featuring a set of preliminary designs centred around the city's Viking past, the Ha'penny Bridge and abstract renditions of the castles and River Liffey. These designs were used to evaluate the core requirements of what the final symbol should look like and represent and led to the final accepted design of the three simplified castles as the new symbol.

Dublin City
Baile Átha Cliath

Above: Almost there...
One of the short-listed designs
which evolved into the
accepted logo, right.

Above: The accepted Dublin City logo along with its
names in English and Irish and the relative proportions
and spacing that must be followed.

Left: The Corporate Identity Manual is designed to brief
users on how the new logo should be implemented
across a wide range of corporate applications.

264

Right: The Dublin City Council logo was revised in 2015
and the new version is designed to ensure that both the Irish
and English text now have equal prominence. This was implemented as
the Irish looked subordinate to the English and the words 'Dublin City' was seen
as branding the city as a whole rather than the council itself. The Three Castles
have also been redesigned to be more equal in size and are now grouped closer
together in a linear format while retaining the original colours for consistency.

**Comhairle Cathrach
Bhaile Átha Cliath
Dublin City Council**

H. M. S. DUBLIN

OBEDIENTIA CIVIUM URBIS FELICITAS

DUBLIN
1907

SHELBOURNE FOOTBALL CLUB
1895

I.A.B.A.
Avona
Boxing Club

QUEEN'S OWN ROYAL REGIMENT

DUBLIN BOY SCOUTS

DUBLIN AND SOUTH EASTERN RAILWAY

át-cliat-dublinne

CITY OF DUBLIN
BATTALION

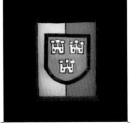

City Arms, Dublin.

Acknowledgments

The Author would like to thank the following individuals and organisations who supplied artifacts, material, histories, artwork and other information. Without their help this book would not have been possible.

An Garda Síochána Museum
An Post & General Post Office
Avona Boxing Club

Bankers Pub, Dame Street
Andrew Bennett
Paul Bommer
Sharon Bowers
Leo Burdock's

Ciara Cantwell
Central Bank of Ireland
Christ Church Cathedral
City Hall, Dublin
Dr. Mary Clark and the Staff, Dublin
  City Library & Archives, Pearse St.
Commercial Rowing Club
Creative Inc. Design
William Crofton

DMOD Architects
DSPCA
Dublin City Council
Dublin City Council Libraries
Dublin Coroner's Court
Dublin Fire Brigade Museum
Dublin Ink, Tattooists
Dublin Intitute of Technology (DIT)
Dublin Naturalists Field Club
Dublin Parks Department
Dublin Wheelers, Cycling Club

Austin Fennessy
  Irish Historical Militaria
Fitzwilliam Square Association

GAA Museum, Croke Park
Georges Street Arcade, Dublin
Glucksman Map Library, Trinity College
Paul Goulding
Gresham Hotel Dublin
Iarnród Éireann - Irish Rail
Irish Museum of Modern Art
Irish Transport Museum, Howth
Kenilworth Bowling Club
King's Hospital School Palmerstown
Sean Harrington Architects
Stg. Colum Kelly
Hugh Lane Gallery, Dublin
Lansdowne Football Club
Mansion House, Dublin
Niall McCormack
Susan McKeever
Merrion Cricket Club
National Library of Ireland
National Print Museum, Dublin
New Ireland Assurance
NTR plc
Óglaigh na hÉireann - Defence Forces
  Ireland & Military Archives
Saint Patrick's Cathedral
Premier Dairies
Simon Prunty of James Fox & Co.
Royal Dublin Fusilliers Association
Royal Dublin Society
Royal Navy, UK
Tony Schorman, Lír Coins & Collectables
Patrick Scott Estate
Scouting Ireland - Dublin Boy Scouts
Alastair Smeaton
South Dublin County Libraries
South Dublin County Council
Sportsfile
Universitiy College Dublin (UCD)
Whitefriars Church, Dublin

269

Bibliography

Arnold, Bruce • Irish Art: A Concise History - Thames & Hudson 1977

Becker, Annette; Wang, Wilfried •
  20th Century Architecture: Ireland - Munich 1997

Beckett, J C • The Making of Modern Ireland 1603–1923 - Faber & Faber 1966

Barnard, T. C • Grand Metropolis or The Anus of the World?
  The Cultural Life of 18th Century Dublin.

Bartlett, Thomas • Ireland: A History - Cambridge University Press 2010

Boran, Pat • A short history of Dublin - Mercier Press

Boyd, Gary A • Dublin, 1745-1922: Hospitals, spectacle and vice -
  Four Courts Press

Brady, Joseph; Anngret Simms • Dublin: through space and time (c. 900-1900
  Four Courts Press

Collin, James • Life in Old Dublin, James Duffy and Co., Dublin 1913.
  Chapters of Dublin History

Carroll, Joseph T • Ireland in the War Years 1939–1945 - International
  Scholars Publishers, San Francisco 2002

Connolly, S.J. • The Oxford Companion to Irish History -
  Oxford University Press 2007

Connor, Dylan; Mills, Gerald; Moore-Cherry, Niamh • The 1911 Census and
  Dublin city: A spatial analysis.

Craig, Maurice James • Dublin, 1660-1860 - Penguin

Craig, Maurice • The Architecture of Ireland from the Earliest Times to 1880
  Batsford 1989

Crokepark.ie • Croke Park Facts and figures.

Dickson, David • The State of Dublin's History Éire-Ireland 2010

Dorney, John • Casualties of the Civil War in Dublin The Irish Story

Dublin City Council • Facts about Dublin City. Dublin.ie

Dublinks.com • Fords & Black Pools -
  History of Dublin Dublin History and Heritage

Dublin Historical Record vol.46 1993

Dublin Protestant Operative Association • Loyal Dublin The Irish Story

Duffy, Sean • A Concise History of Ireland, 2005

Edwards, Ruth • An Atlas of Irish History - Routledge 2005

Fagan, Patrick • The Population of Dublin in the Eighteenth Century -
  Iris an dá chultúr,

Foster, Robert Fitzroy • Modern Ireland, 1600–1972 - Penguin Books 1988.

Geoghegan, Patrick • Liberator, The Life and Death of Daniel O'Connell

Hanna, Erika • Dublin's North Inner City, Preservationism, and Irish Modernity
  in the 1960s - Historical Journal 2010

Index

Hanna, Erika • Modern Dublin: Urban Change and the Irish Past, 1957-1973
Oxford University Press, 2013

Igoe, Brian • The Story of Ireland 2009

Independent Newspapers

Irish Times Newspaper

Jacobsen, John • Chasing Progress in the Irish Republic
Cambridge University Press 1994

Joyce, P.W. • A Concise History of Ireland

Kee, Robert • The Green Flag: A History of Irish Nationalism
Weidenfeld and Nicholson London 1972

Kilfeather, Siobhán Marie • Dublin: A cultural history
Oxford University Press 2005.

Lennon, Colm; Montague, John • John Rocque's Dublin
A Guide to the Georgian City - Royal Irish Academy, 2010

Liddy, Pat • Dublin A Celebration From the 1st to the 21st century
Dublin City Council, 2000

Lyons, F.S.L • Ireland since the famine - Collins/Fontana 1973

McCarthy, Denis; Benton, David • Dublin Castle: at the heart of Irish History
Government Stationery Office 2004

McDonald, Frank • Saving the City: How to Halt the Destruction of Dublin
Tomar Publishing, 1989

McManus, Ruth • Dublin, 1910-1940: Shaping the city & suburbs
Four Courts Press, 2002

McParland, Edward • Public Architecture in Ireland 1680–1760
Yale University Press, 2001

Mokyr, Joel; Ó Gráda, Cormac • New Developments in Irish Population History,
1700-1850 - The Economic History Review

Murphy, James H • Ireland: a social, cultural and literary history, 1791-1891
Four Courts Press, 2003

Murphy, John A • Ireland in the Twentieth Century - Gill & Macmillan

Ó Gráda, Cormac • A Rocky Road: The Irish Economy Since the 1920s
Manchester University Press 1997

Ó Gráda, Cormac • The Great Irish Famine - Cambridge University Press 1989

Prunty, Jacinta • Dublin slums, 1800-1925: a study in urban geography - Irish
Academic Press, 1998

Ryan, Rev. J • Pre-Norman Dublin

Taoiseach, Department of • Guide to Government Buildings 2005

Stokes, Margaret • Early Christian art in Ireland - Chapman & Hall, London 1888

www.libraryireland.com

www.wikipedia.com

270

Index

You'll find them everywhere.

Examples of water hydrant pavement covers featuring
the three castles and found in Ballydehob, West Cork,
over 350 kilometres from Dublin.

I hope you enjoyed the book but I'll admit I've probably missed a few. I'm always on the lookout for more examples of Dublin's heraldic achievements, coats of arms and symbols featuring the three castles. If you do come across a set of them, be it on a building, in a book or on the ground and that hasn't been listed in the book I'd be very grateful if you could make a note of it, even take a photo and send on the details to me at: *threecastlesofdublin@gmail.com*

Your help is much appreciated. Many thanks.

The Glovers & Skinners Arms

The Goldsmiths Arms

The Curriers Painters Stainers &
Stationers Arms

The Curriers Arms

The Weavers Arms

The Coopers Arms

The Bricklayers & Plasterers Arms

The Brewers & Maltsters Arms

The Shearmen & Dyers Arms

The Felt Makers Arms

The Hosiers Arms

The Joyners Arms

PUPILS

PUPILS

AN EYE-OPENING ACCOUNT
OF MEDICAL PRACTICE
WITHOUT STANDARDS

BERNARD J. SUSSMAN, M.D.

FOREWORD BY JAMES H. SCHEUER

Bartleby Press
Silver Spring, Maryland

Printed in the United States of America

Published by:

Bartleby Press
11141 Georgia Avenue
Silver Spring, MD 20902

www.BartlebythePublisher.com

Library of Congress Cataloging-in-Publication Data

Sussman, Bernard J.
 Pupils : an eye-opening account of medical practice without standards
/ Bernard J. Sussman.
    p. ; cm.
 ISBN 0-910155-49-6 (alk. paper)
1. Neurosurgeons—Malpractice. 2. Physicians—Malpractice. 3.
Medical errors.
    [DNLM: 1. Medical Errors. 2. Neurosurgery—standards. 3.
Dilatation. 4. Malpractice. 5. Pupil. WL 368 S964p 2003] I. Title.

 RD593.S88 2003
 344.73'04121—dc21
                                    2003002542

In Memory of
Valentino D.B. Mazzia

American Medical Association
Principles of Medical Ethics

§II. *A physician shall uphold the standards of professionalism, be honest in all professional interactions, and strive to report physicians deficient in character or competence, or engaged in fraud or deception, to appropriate entities.*

Contents

Foreword

PUPILS is not just another medical horror story served up to exploit the public appetite for sensational accounts of irresponsible or errant doctors. With his considerable experience as clinician, professor, research scientist, and forensic expert in neurosurgery, Doctor Sussman has studied a number of cases of medical negligence and come to a conclusion which I find difficult to challenge. Simply stated, it is that the profession of medicine, oddly enough, is not being held to any specific standards.

In my own state of New York, for example, the Department of Health was recently forced for the first time to set a standard for the performance of a surgical procedure. It did so because seven patients have died and 185 have suffered serious complications from laparoscopic gall bladder surgery in 99 of New York's 242 hospitals since August of 1990. The situation had become so critical that incidences of complications were being reported at the rate of three or four per week. And why? Because doctors were never required, either by their colleagues or hospitals, to learn how to perform this surgery properly.

It is Dr. Sussman's opinion that it is possible to set reasonable standards for most of what doctors do. He presents cogent and persuasive arguments for setting such standards in the closing pages of this book.

Surely everyone agrees that all Americans should have quality medical and surgical care. With that in mind, Congress has looked at the various ways by which such care can be guaranteed by law. It is my belief that a nationally funded single payer plan is the most promising and logical approach; for one thing, it offers the best prospect of underwriting and implementing the kinds of medical standards that Doctor Sussman advocates. Taxpayers have the right to know that their money is properly spent and that the services they receive are appropriately defined.

The setting of medical guidelines has been considered by the Congressional Subcommittee on Health. This committee has proposed a new agency for the study of the outcomes of medical procedures. Guidelines for the management of pain are its first achievement. Upcoming panels may provide similar guidelines for the treatment of urinary incontinence in adults, sickle cell anemia, depression, lower back pain, and other afflictions. Of course, because they are unenforceable, such guidelines are only a start. It remains for us to come to grips with the need to assure safe, reliable, and effective medical and surgical procedures. If the medical profession had moved years ago to set for itself the kinds of standards for which Doctor Sussman now argues, the tragic results of inadequate treatment would have in most cases been prevented.

Doctor Sussman offers a visionary approach to the future of medicine while advocating ways to cope with current problems. I am particularly impressed by his prediction that many of the answers to our present problems will come by way of medical automation. While I believe that there will always be a need for human and personal interaction between doctor and patient, I have come to believe that computer assisted or directed diagnosis and treatment are the wave of the medical future.

But we live in the present, not the future. And this author confronts us here with the mind-boggling reality of a profession that holds our lives in trust, yet is not accountable for meeting any specific standards. It is high time that we move in the direction Doctor Sussman advocates: the standardization and availability of the best medical care that we have to offer. Such a move will result in the continuing upgrading of the practice of medicine and will rescue it from its present status as just another haphazard entrepreneurial endeavor. It will become what was originally intended, a true profession, one devoted to doctors giving honest and dedicated service to their patients.

James H. Scheuer
Former Member, U.S. House of Representatives,
8th District, New York

Preface

This book is intended for any person concerned about receiving good medical or surgical treatment, and a natural preoccupation it is. Even I, though a physician with certain privileges and knowledge not available to everyone, have worried about whether or not my family and I would receive adequate care should we need it. On occasion, I have had my own difficulties in this regard. But by being scrupulously selective, I've generally succeeded. Unfortunately, those who are not doctors nor so diligently discriminating, are less apt to be as lucky as I have been. And those two exceptions, when other doctors let me down, stick in my mind.

Most Americans worry more about health insurance coverage than they do about the services such insurance obtains. There has been little concentrated study of the fact that medical and surgical services are commonly uneven and unreliable, and that these services are performed by very well paid physicians *who are not held to any clearly stated standards for their practice of medicine.* Worse yet, poor people who have no health insurance seem to receive woefully inadequate treatment. That is not to say the wealthy are not also frequently victimized by health care providers.

Compounding the dilemma for rich and poor, young and old, is the advent of managed care, health maintenance insurance, and systems both federal and private, under which reimbursements to both hospitals and doctors encourage the provision of a kind of medical care which is often not only minimal or marginal but can be unsafe, if not dangerous. Now, why should all of these things be so?

It has become this writer's conviction that no satisfactory answer to such questions can be obtained from further study of general statistics or some newly detailed data base. Such a broad overview of the subject is what someone like myself, trained in the medical discipline, would be inclined to label the "gross" findings, a mere starting point of any useful inquiry. This problem calls for a more detailed, even "microscopic" examination.

That sort of study must inevitably lead to an evaluation of the actual purveyors of health care, the doctors, and we must ask: Why is it that doctors often fail to act in a patient's best interest? Why are they neither held to a requirement of conformity to stipulated standards for their clinical actions nor made consistently accountable should they treat their patients in ways that are not acceptable?

It should be obvious that there is little to be learned from a study of doctors' successes. Only a detailed examination of their individual failures can supply the necessary information. But the problem here is that doctors only occasionally acknowledge their failures, and even when such failures are reported they are buried in hospital-based accounts of complications and deaths not accessible to the public. Furthermore, should these adverse results surface in hospital conferences, they are likely to be glossed over, if not condoned. It is also the case that under current law, what has been discussed in such proceedings is often protected. It cannot be disclosed. Lastly, there is the problem that because doctors, as we're so constantly told, are only human and subject to human error, it becomes too easy to excuse them for unacceptable performance and too hard for them, in turn, to be objective or critical of one another's lapses. The result is a close-mouthed discipline, with doctors protecting their mutual interests, the so-called conspiracy of silence operating in a climate of public forbearance.

The issue of human medical errors surfaced most recently (November 29, 1999) in a report from the Institute of Medicine, an arm of the National Academy of Sciences. It alleges that as many as 98,000 Americans die unnecessarily each year because of medical mistakes made by physicians, pharmacists, and other health care professionals. These are the negligent acts that are due to things like illegible prescriptions written by doctors, wrong vial selections by nurses, improper dose selections by pharmacists, wrong leg amputations, and other acts of simple carelessness, matters having nothing to do with the problem I am addressing but which I suspect will be seized upon to divert attention from, or to offer nonviable excuses for, the much greater problem of there being no controlling standards for the practice of medicine.

So how can we make an in-depth study of what is strictly the issue of professional failures on the part of individual physicians?

There is only one way to the information needed—the patients themselves, who have filed formal charges against doctors and hospitals, or whose families have done so. In other words, a study of the substance of representative medical malpractice claims that have gone to court.

In this book I have made such a study. It is an offering based upon fifty-one years of experience as medical student, intern, resident, medical specialist, researcher and teacher, as well as more than thirty-four years of experience reviewing several hundred files of alleged medical malpractice. It is my conclusion that when medical care is inadequate it is because doctors are indeed all too "human." Unfortunately, they seem to be incorrigibly so. And thus far their efforts to monitor, police, or even discipline themselves have failed to curb this "humanity." Moreover, they have yet to conclude, much less even grudgingly concede, that they should be governed by reasonably set standards for the care they render.

What our medical future will or can be, and how patients and society may move to cope with this problem are what I shall discuss here, drawing upon instances of malpractice litigation with which I have become familiar. I have also chosen to comment briefly upon managed health care, a system oriented toward rewarding doctors financially for taking quite unnecessary chances with their patients and putting them at ill-advised risk.

It is not my purpose to harass any particular physicians. I choose rather to focus my attention on the consequences of their practicing medicine out of accordance with any set of stipulated standards. Therefore, I shall not identify any of these examples of medical or surgical deviation as known matters of official record or by other reference. Names and locations have been disguised so as to protect the guilty, and irrelevant details have been altered so that no implications regarding any particular physician should be assumed by the reader. This book, however, has been inspired by the improper care rendered by these doctors. If in a sense it reads like a work of fiction, it's a fiction based upon truths I consider to be obvious and important to the education not only of the public, but of legislators, lawyers, and hopefully the medical profession.

As for truth, I have often been struck by what happens in one of its ultimate moments. At times of death resulting from severe increase in pressure within the cranial cavity, caused either by an untreatable condition or because proper care has not been forthcoming, the pupils commonly dilate. It has always seemed to me that what is being projected at that moment is a wide-eyed awareness of death's imminence. In one instance it could be attributed to fright. In another, perhaps, a reaction to the injustice of being so unfairly treated or neglected. Of course, this is only something I have fancied, but these thoughts linger enough that I build my case regarding medical negligence and medical mismanagement precisely on those circumstances associated with such critical and terminal medical events.

1

Maverick Professor

The assailant was never identified. The victim, a young
black salesman, was seated in his car studying route as-
signments when he turned in the direction of something
that had caught his eye. The bullet, fired into his mouth, shat-
tered several teeth, lacerated his tongue, and lodged in the right
tonsil. Still conscious, he was rushed to the nearest hospital.
That bright day, supposed to launch him modestly but still
proudly into the first semblance of something like a real career,
would carry him, instead, to his end. The price for having the
audacity to go where some would say he did not belong. There
was no other reason that such a person should be set upon so
savagely.

The ambulance drivers were decent enough. They took
him quickly to the closest hospital, a private institution, even
though black people would ordinarily be driven somewhat
farther down the road to a county hospital. It would be the
only accommodation extended him that day. Whether it had
to do with genuine concern for his medical condition or the
imminent and unpleasant prospect of his dying aboard their
ambulance is uncertain, given the place and the time of the
event.

A nose and throat specialist was summoned to the emergency room. Finding the bullet to be embedded in the tonsil,
that doctor reached into the victim's throat with a long curved
surgical clamp and pulled the bullet free. He flipped it into
a bedside basin where it clattered to a stop. A narcotic and
a tranquilizer were ordered to be given by injection. What
next? Careful further examination to see if the carotid artery,

located just behind the tonsil, was pulsing and carrying blood to the right side of the patient's brain? Some kind of clinical action out of regard for obvious weakness of this man's left arm and leg, indication that, in fact, the carotid artery was so injured? Admission to the secluded area reserved for just a few black patients that he might be observed for delayed bleeding? No. The young wife and other relatives now present were advised to take him to their dentist's office so that fractured teeth could be extracted and his mouth cleansed. That was deemed better than to admit him to the hospital and to have a consulting, presumably white dentist, come and treat him.

Those frightened people complied. They carried him off, he by then drowsy and limp, to a black dentist who could not understand why anyone "in such god-awful condition," with head thrown back, was to be found sprawling in his treatment chair. He summoned another ambulance, the drivers of which, sizing up the situation, risked the trip of greater distance and transported him to the county hospital. It was there that he died a few days later, untreated for the blood clot in his carotid artery, and the secondary effects of that occlusive injury upon his brain. Specialists who did charitable consultations at that hospital did them too infrequently and too poorly to be of much help to a black patient with such urgent medical needs.

This patient should have had an immediate neurosurgical consultation at the first hospital. He needed an emergency x-ray study of his carotid artery, an arteriogram, to document that it had been occluded by a clot or a swelling type injury. And he required immediate surgery to restore blood flow to the brain by whatever technique seemed feasible at the time of surgical exploration. If such treatment had been required by an operating standard and had been rendered, the patient would have survived and in all likelyhood recovered. But there is no such standard.

Some people want to die in their own beds and among their own kind. If that was this man's wish, it was at least half-honored.

The bullet which ended this man's life caused my own to change. Just a few years later, in 1969, I would find myself seated in a courtroom alongside a young attorney from the NAACP. My job was to give expert testimony, as a neurosurgeon, that the dead man had been the victim, ultimately, of medical malpractice. His, was to show that the treatment was compromised out of racially biased motives. It was my second year at Howard University College of Medicine, where I would become Professor of Neurosurgery. The lawyer, Mr. Julius Chambers, would later serve the NAACP with distinction as its lead counsel and argue cases before the Supreme Court. The result of our joint efforts hardly augured that well for either of our careers.

The case was lost. The single black person on that jury wrote me subsequently to say that there had never been a chance of our prevailing, but that she "sure appreciated your trying."

Since that was the situation, it has always been hard for me to comprehend why anyone had bothered to make threatening calls to me in Washington, to the extent that during trial I had to spend my nights sequestered outside of town in the home of a certain gentleman, both sympathetic and well enough armed to deal with the promise of someone "ready to shoot the ass off any guy coming down here who doesn't mind his own damned business." As it turned out, a black civil rights attorney and an outsider Jewish doctor were certainly no serious threat to well-established persons in that jurisdiction. I suppose, however, that there are those who are as much offended by the charge and the talk of discriminatory practices as by the prospect of really being held to account for them.

That case and, later, others, were referred to me by professors at Howard University employed in the law and medical schools. I had the feeling, at the time, that for certain university administrators, I was even fancied to be some sort of great white hope for such adversarial matters. In me, it seemed, they had their own white credentialed person to argue, if need be, against his like peers around the country. Even though this sat well enough with me in the beginning, as time passed, I would come to resent that no black professor ever felt behooved to make common cause with me. It was as if they had more to lose than I did in supporting charges of medical malpractice and civil rights abuse. While such African American doctors curried the favor of their white professional colleagues and remained in good professional grace in the interest of their own careers, I was eased into the role of maverick neurosurgical professor, the outsider who could be counted upon to buck the system.

As things turned out, it was a simple matter for me to quickly become quite notorious. In the specialty of neurological surgery, more than in any other clinical field of medical practice, doctors are disinclined to criticize a colleague. And because neurosurgical malpractice is as widespread as it is in any other clinical field, there happen to be many lawyers nationwide having great difficulty in making credible and viable charges of this kind stick, simply for lack of supportive expert testimony. Should there be only a few doctors willing to speak out, it will not be long before those physicians are well known to lawyers specializing in this kind of work. It will also happen that just as quickly, such assertive rank breaking physicians will draw both the attention and the ire of their medical colleagues. As time passed, I became involved not only in those cases of neurosurgical injury associated with racial discrimination, but also in circumstances where the only issues were those of substandard medical practice. The transition was easy enough because I had become increasingly indignant and curious about what was being uncovered.

Over a period of thirty years I studied the hospital records of hundreds of patients. I also examined their x-rays, their laboratory reports, and the sworn testimony of the doctors who treated them and of the medical experts who testified in their behalf. Often, matters of a personal nature also came to light. There were doctors with inadequate training or education, problems with addiction, even drug trafficking and criminal offenses that, on occasion, had been expunged from police records. Most of the neurosurgeons, however, had impeccable qualifications.

More often than not it was my opinion that the charge of malpractice had no merit. Under that circumstance, I made every effort to persuade the attorney referring the matter for my review to drop charges. Sometimes I succeeded. Of the cases I considered to have merit, if the malpractice was flagrant and the damage to the patient severe, I generally agreed to testify in support of the plaintiff's claim. There were only a few situations in which I was called upon to defend the actions of a neurosurgeon against the accusation of malpractice. For a long time this puzzled me. It was certainly only in part explained by the fact of there being absolutely no shortage of doctors willing to defend other doctors. That is so even when the medical care has been egregious. I finally settled on the suspicion that if defense lawyers could no longer ask me in court the presumably embarrassing question of why, almost always, it was an injured patient that I testified for, rather than some doctor, they would lose an advantage they fancied to have over me. In all likelihood theirs was a joint strategy worked out between them and various insurance companies representing doctors or hospitals.

So by the chance of my employment at a university committed to civil rights issues, and my own inclination to object to medical injuries stemming from racism, I came, over time, to have a privileged view of how my own specialty, that of neurological surgery, was actually being practiced just about everywhere. It was a shocking perspective. Things were definitely not what I had previously assumed. For here was not the kind of care one would suppose from articles published either in medical journals or newspapers. But it was happening. And it took prying into the records of patients who had suffered at the hands of their doctors to find it out. The scientific papers being published out of prestigious institutions would lead one to believe that such things could not and did not occur. And yet, I found myself reading of situations wherein eminent professors were cornered on the witness stand and forced to admit otherwise. Astoundingly, bad, even tragic results, the obvious consequence of substandard care, were either being falsely characterized or omitted entirely from certain otherwise glowing claims to be found in the medical literature. You would never know such things if you practiced medicine in a small New Jersey community as I had before moving to Washington. But from 1967 on I was able to scan my specialty across the country and soon was able to see how unseemly it could often be. That is not to say that great things were not also being accomplished by neurosurgeons. They were. The problem was that too much of what was happening was unacceptable. I testfied more and more often.

A neurosurgeon who would help injured patients by testifying in their behalf, and who could do so with the credentials of a full-time professor, was assured of instant notoriety in both medical and legal professional circles. Neurosurgical societies, in particular, looked upon these activities of mine with opprobrium, and with the assistance of insurance companies offering malpractice coverage to doctors, began to collect, print, advertise and put out for sale, complete transcripts of my testimony as given before trial or in court. By adding this measure to the prevailing conspiracy of silence regarding neurosurgical malpractice, there came about a kind of backroom intrigue for defense lawyers, insurance companies, and professional organizations to collaborate, ostensibly making it easier to crossexamine me as the occasions arose. Thus, my opinions on a wide variety of medico-legal issues became very well documented, published, and circulated.

It also came about, however, that I could no longer find an audience or a forum for my purely academic scientific opinions. Medical articles I'd authored were turned back by the editors of leading journals, or were accepted, and then somehow never managed to find their way into print.

Professional societies refused me the opportunity to present the results of my research; indeed, on one occasion, when through some oversight I was scheduled to speak, that invitation was withdrawn because a colleague had objected. It did not matter that I had invented a new technique for removing herniated discs safely with an enzyme, as an alternative to surgery. It did not matter that I had previously published articles on brain oxygen tension which incorporated new concepts and provided new terminology for the scientific literature. No one even chose to remember any longer that earlier in my career I had pioneered the use of an enzyme for the purpose of removing blood clots and unblocking arteries in patients with stroke, establishing a basis for current treatment of that type in patients having either heart attacks or strokes. I was now a pariah of the neurosurgical community and anything else about me was erased from its collective memory.

The last articles I did manage to publish were not in neurosurgical journals at all but in the Journal of the American Medical Association and an English Journal, Paraplegia. Fortunately, in this way, as by an opportune backdoor, I was able to get into print some research results and to at least publish my reasons for having said what I had testified to in court about several instances of neurosurgical malpractice which involved spine and spinal cord injury. But for me to catalog, document, and analyze that sort of thing in a scientific paper and to critique what had been the professional reaction to it, was taken by my colleagues as the ultimate of my affronts.

For a neurosurgeon to suggest but once, even timidly, that some other neurosurgeon has erred, is already to be outrageous and to be universally condemned. It is also considered to be forever unforgivable. There is not much difference between the hatred of an Ayatollah Khomeini for a Salman Rushdie and that of organized neurosurgery for a colleague who testifies against other neurosurgeons, other than the publicly stated verdict and grim sentence in the

Iranian instance, as against the clandestine malevolence of professional organizations. It was utterly unimaginable to neurosurgeons that one of their own, and a professor to boot, could become so increasingly vocal to the point even, of appearing belligerent. But why should I not be so, if I was right? Mine were serious and important allegations needing to be made about circumstances that were appalling. And more often than not those who defended such care, doctors and lawyers both, were lying and damned well knew it! But might there not be coy, or gentle, the so-called understated and constructive ways of saying much the same things, but outside of courtrooms, and wind up having my perceptions better received, even acted upon? Not a chance. Besides which, who else was there to support the claims of all of these injured patients? And finally, on a personal level, what could I possibly gain by desisting from further testimony, even were I to consider that irresponsible option? There was no way I could ever hope to be well regarded again professionally, much less make academic progress. Neurosurgical excommunication is total and permanent. Any professor who makes waves is anathema to the neurosurgical community, everywhere in this country. And as it turned out, that would even be the case at my own university. For in due time self-appointed neurosurgical emissaries turned up at my department chairman's office urging that I be dumped.

Also, at my university, it just so happened that there had emerged a disposition to abandon traditional politics of protest, to forego militancy, and to join the mainstream. As that change of overall focus and purpose developed I could sense local embarrassment regarding my continued activities in the medico-legal sphere. Howard University could possibly ill afford my tenured presence if now its aims were to "overcome" merely by going along. And by all that I could discern, those persons in charge seemed to feel, in spite of having drawn me into this messy business in the first place, that they owed me nothing! Academic memories extend no further than do any others. Actually, it was only my tenured status that in the end saved me.

But to become then, isolated, shunned, resented, probably as much at my own institution as by those I had faulted elsewhere for lapses of their medical staffs, was to occasion still another turning point for what had become a maverick professor. Awareness of the self serving, narrow minded prevailing antagonism toward me provoked an odd shift in my reading of the situation. For what to me had heretofore represented the tumultuous emotional field revolving about very specialized medical or scientific issues and controversies began to strike me as having the mark of a different and more fundamental phenomenon, something quite apart the everyday sort of furor engendered by technically oriented medical disputes. These various medical and surgical tragedies I had been confronted with had a unitary, highly energized root and it ran much deeper than that of doctors incompetent by chance, irresponsible as flawed beginners, or overwhelmed as doddering seniors, culprits all and shielded by their all-too-willing unscrupulous lawyers. To the contrary, this was about a peculiar, often latent and dark, but essential side of human nature. It is the basis for problems we have more serious than medical negligence, but it is there also. And then there was the obvious pressing question. Could that self-devoted, aggressive, often brutish element of the human persona, the part ignored by most discussions of "humanism," ever be reasonably and unrestrictedly entrusted with the care of other human lives? Because we do as much, unavoidably, with our doctors. It had finally dawned upon me, under the pressures of having to endure an increasingly stressful, adversarial existence, that I was entirely off the mark. I had spent too many years bewailing avoidable clinical tragedies and castigating medical troublemakers by the numbers, all the while completely unmindful of the primary cause of so much of that professional chaos. As it turned out, deviant medical practice was integral to the behavioral habitudes of those doctors I had complained about. Being ingrained, it was impervious to criticism, and certainly beyond all possibility of influence by my or anyone else's aggrieved grumbling, however unrelenting.

In the last and most relevant kind of analysis, the one a straightforward and unsophisticated person might come up with, medical negligence, substandard care, and the animated struggle to protect those responsible for it, were simply evils. With one simplistic but enlightened leap, such a person could come closer to the reality of the problem than I had during all my years of meticulous, subterranean probing.

Is that a strange posture for a neurosurgeon to assume by way of final pronouncement upon certain aspects of his profession? Can I call it something, anything, else? I cannot put it any other way. Medical negligence and everything associated with it is an evil. How else to label what I have witnessed and examined for so long? How else to comprehend the futility of all conceivable efforts for undoing this commonplace professional inclination by mere opposition? What else can I call the innumerable unnecessary risks taken both by doctors and health care administrators with the sick, the self-serving desertions by doctors of their patients, the expressions of hostility by health care providers, the damaging effects all concerned have had upon vulnerable patients, and ultimately, the bold-faced defense of what has been perpetrated? What good comes of excusing it as being "only human" or as some self-aggrandizing kind of human motivation driven irresistibly by genes, hormones, or insistent cellular drive centers within the brain, all of it brought about by the forces of evolution? It is more to the point to just call it what everyone should be able to understand, an evil.

Such evil, like any other, cannot be directly influenced. The ways, origins, and the effects of evil, however, can be described, understood, and hopefully circumvented. It seems to me that the evil of substandard medical care can possibly be limited or even thwarted by simply having a handle on its real nature. Then one is able to attempt an appropriate remedy. The remedy I propose would counter the all too human inclinations responsible for medical negligence by imposing a range of accepted and strict standards for medical conduct in most clinical circumstances.

If we examine just a few cases of neurosurgical malpractice, selected for no reason other than that they bear the common stamp of a particular physical finding usually held to override all other neurosurgical clinical concerns, my thesis can be looked at. These are patients who at one point or another developed a wide dilatation of the pupil. And even if some readers should find my conclusions suspect, the subject of pupillary dilatation is significant and its study a reward in itself.

2

The Pupil

Certain women who dote on appearing beautiful consider eyes more fetching if the pupils are dilated. Psychological studies have shown that men, although ignorant on such matters, nevertheless consistently prefer from among otherwise identical photographs, those female countenances having dilated pupils. It would appear that enlarged pupils are appreciated instinctually or intuitively as indicators of sexual excitement.

There was even a time when women used eye drops to enlarge the pupils. Those drops contained atropine, a chemical which blocks the action of another substance known as acetyl choline, elaborated at the nerve fiber endings of the oculomotor or third cranial nerve at their points of contact with the pupillary musculature. Since the action of acetyl choline is contraction of the pupillary sphincter muscle to produce pupillary constriction, such instillation of atropine prevents that effect, and causes pupillary dilatation. Solutions of atropine came actually to be known as "Bella Donna," the "beautiful woman." A curious matter that women, trying to enhance their appearance, should produce an effect strongly simulating one of the clinical signs and omens of impending death: the fixed and dilated pupil.

The pupil of the eye provides an apperceptive portal to the seen world. It consists of a black, rounded void covered by a transparent bubble, the cornea, and its size is shaped by the encircling muscle of the iris, which contains the various pigments that determine its color. Pupils vary continuously in size as the muscle of the pupillary sphincter reacts to a delicately adjusted balance of local nerve impulses and chemical substances travelling to it via the blood stream.

The most common alteration in size of the pupil is produced by its response to light. As bright light passes through the pupil, it falls upon the photosensitive back wall of the eyeball, the retina. A nerve signal is then generated which is conducted by the optic nerve to the midbrain, a vital upper part of the brain stem connecting the higher brain or cerebrum to the lower brain stem and spinal cord. That signal activates a nerve center in the midbrain, which in its turn transmits an impulse over the adjacent oculomotor nerve. Action of that nerve causes the pupil to narrow, much as the opening in a camera lens is reduced in size to reduce the amount of light reaching the film plane. In the case of the eye it is the amount of light falling upon the retina which is thereby lessened. Alterations in the size of the pupil are also made as an "accommodation" to the need for looking at objects at various distances. The brain is clued to that need by signals from the ciliary muscle which serves the focusing function of adjusting the curvature of the ocular lens.

When a person is beset by strong emotions, such as excitement, anger, or fear, the pupils enlarge in response to the influence of another nerve pathway known as the sympathetic nervous system. This system delivers nerve fibers up into the cranial cavity by way of the carotid artery as it winds its way upward through the neck. Carried to the eye alongside a branch of that artery, the sympathetic fibers cause the pupils to dilate. The pupils may also enlarge as part of a generalized body reaction to some crisis when adrenaline, a hormone, is released into the blood stream by the adrenal gland. This release also causes maximal arousal and alertness, increased heart rate, and reduction of blood flow to certain organs not needed in an emergency. The individual becomes prepared for either "fight or flight" in order to survive a challenge to its existence. Adrenaline-like substances can also be instilled into the eye to produce pupillary dilatation. Thus, the size of the pupils at any particular time results from a continuous interplay of various influences.

Clearly, the pupils may be an important indicator of a threatening environment. And in this way man resembles any other animal trapped in its lair, lashing out in deliberate or blind, frustrated rage, or even frozen immobile in resigned terror.

Alterations in the size of the pupils can also be a sign of serious disease or injuries as they come to affect the central nervous system. In that circumstance, when the pupil enlarges, it is as the result of ominous changes taking place at the very heart of the nervous system, in or near the brain stem, where control centers for the vital life sustaining functions of consciousness, respiration, and blood pressure regulation are located.

Pupillary dilatation can be seen at a glance, so even the ordinary person can learn to tell, just about immediately, if another human, or some lower animal, is putting out this unmistakable signal of emotional stress, serious neurological damage, or imminent death.

But this is not an account of how ordinary persons make that observation. This is, for one thing, about well-educated doctors, specialists in medicine, who for various reasons have either happened or chosen to ignore such signals, or to act inappropriately upon them. Because professional lapses of that kind are usually associated with the most serious of clinical consequences, there is special reason for examining them. And because failure to recognize or to act upon even these most apparent and unmistakable clinical appearances does occur, the question also begs asking: What happens when less obvious signs of abnormality are present, need to be detected, but they are not?

It is the case, moreover, that changes in the pupil have been the clear-cut, occasional result of inappropriate, neglectful, or misdirected treatment. There are surviving patients who carry the stigmata of such injury, sometimes surgical in nature, and their useful lives have been compromised because of the carelessness, ineptitude, or limited knowledge of that kind of physician. Other patients have succumbed. Out of self interest, doctors are not likely to admit that patients die or leave their care bearing the scars of such negligence.

Precisely where or when the events that I shall relate took place is not as important as the fact that they have occurred.

Others, quite like them, have been more frequent than is commonly realized.

When humans, and other animals, make even a nonstressful final passage, the pupils may go briefly to mid dilatation, but those pupils are not being mobilized by some ecstatic vision, nor is it that they muster, however feebly, an insistent last opposition, or register fright for the prospect of oblivion. Then, there is no longer the possibility of resisting or of being afraid. Blood no longer flows to the shaping musculature of the pupil, or to the brain itself, and that musculature is forced to release its hold. The pupil springs open one last time. Nothing is being signified. It is a passive surrender.

3

Harry

STANDARD

Patients or their responsible surrogates should be given full and appropriate descriptions of their therapeutic options and alternatives in advance of treatment for any illness.

There are times when the nurses forget to open his eyes. It hardly matters. Harry can barely see. What little he does is towards the left. For this small advantage, strips of adhesive tape are bridged between his upper eyelids and forehead, to hold his eyes open. When he sweats, the tape peels away, the lids droop again, his eyes close, and the skin irritation from all of that incessant taping and retaping makes him miserable.

Those eyes, exposed in such a rude way, and skewed in opposite directions, jerk about searchingly to create a comical yet pathetic look of bewilderment. When, finally, they do come to rest, their pupils stare widely and do not contract if bright light should happen to fall upon them. More than just the light fails to register behind Harry's enormous dark pupils. He will forget in an instant anyone and anything that may briefly attract his attention, for he has lost the ability to retain and to imprint the memory of recent occurrences. Consequently, he is no longer able to learn. What he can do, however, with what remains of his brain, is recall the distant past and how pleasant it was five years ago, before the operation, when after a bitterly contested divorce proceeding, he happily remarried. He knows, at least, that his present condition is quite different. Seated in his wheelchair, helpless because he cannot see or learn, unable to walk, or even to find his face to scratch it, because of hands which do not feel, and have no sense of their position, he embarrasses every visitor by apologizing for his condition. The surgeon who brought about this calamitous circumstance has neither apologies nor honest explanations.

Before surgery, Harry was uncustomarily talkative. The nurses entered his commentaries into the medical record. Those notations read oddly, poignantly, now. He was full of hope. He spoke unabashedly of the pleasure he had found with his new wife, "a wonderful woman," of being very comfortable with her, of his resolution to spend more time with his children, of new prospects. Then he would digress to describe himself as something of a recluse. During the summer, for example, when he vacationed, it was his habit to travel through New Hampshire and once there to sit beside his camper and read, or fish, or just to sit, enjoying the quietude. But abruptly, on one occasion, this carpenter happened to say, and seemingly quite beside the point: "No one respects or cares about an ordinary working man anymore. It didn't use to be that way." For Harry, that was no more than detached preoperative commentary. If he had been apprehensive about what lay ahead, one might say it was a foreboding. But he felt confident regarding his operation. As events developed, he was, in fact, not at all respected. Not even for the ability to decide how he might be treated. His surgeon took it upon himself to do that for him.

In any case, there was nothing more than ordinary about Harry. His fate, if he had not grown a tumor of the pituitary gland, would have been to slip through life sometimes affably, sometimes angrily, but in general like most people, coping and unnoticed.

All of that changed with the operation. As surgical complications go, his was spectacular. The only reason it did not come to be well known was that it was never brought up for discussion, or review, either at the hospital or in the medical community. Barely a note of its acknowledgement appeared in the hospital chart postoperatively until Harry's surgeon did record, finally, when after two weeks his patient emerged from coma, that there were certain specific neurological "findings" and "deficits." "Findings?" "Deficits?" The appearance of this patient after operation was enough to assault the sensitivities of the most experienced and hardened of clinical observers! After all, before this unfortunate event, no one had ever described the consequence of going through the nose to remove a tumor of the pituitary gland, located beneath the undersurface of the brain, only to plunge beyond a proper depth and drive a surgical instrument into the very tissues of the midbrain. That extraordinarily vital structure is a center for many critical neurological functions. It is also a pathway for connections between all of them.

Consultants were finally called, even distinguished emeritus professors, who asserted obligingly, that such clinical signs as were manifest could not possibly be directly related to the surgery. Physicians who had written learned medical treatises couched in specific scientific terminology, highly regarded for its exactitude, now talked about "disturbances" and anaesthetic "problems" related to low oxygen tension or high blood pressure, when there was no evidence from the medical record that trends involving such changes had transpired. The hospital chart became little more than a repository for defensive vagaries and obfuscations.

Six months later, the wife, in Harry's behalf, would file suit against the neurosurgeon. The legal battle which ensued involved famous physicians, prominent medical institutions, leading law firms, and professors retained as experts for both sides, drawn from medical centers across the country. Even so, the public took no notice. There was no media attention because such contests have become everyday matters in an adversarial world. They are mere ritualized mind clashes, not conflicts about anything substantive, and are acted out reflexively. Even the lawyers are bored by much of it. They put in their time for lucre and devotedly attend the clock, not the serious questions that might be raised when tragedies like this take place. And the final results of such litigation do not lay any serious claim to anybody's attention, either. There is surely no public understanding of what has actually happened. It is only on infrequent occasion that the participating lawyers even

believe in the roles they play or in the positions they have
staked out. And those doctors having knowledge or suspicion
of the unfortunate reality at the core of all of this travail, by
virtue of their involvement in the patient's medical care, their
acquaintance with the defendant doctor, or their being retained
as defense experts, never do express it. That is a matter which
cannot be admitted or discussed. It is kept secret. It may also
never come to be understood or charged by the plaintiff. Such
lawsuits, invariably, are about the technical aspect of deviations
from legally (not medically) defined accepted standards, and
do not address the all too commonly uncontrollable and inappropriate behavior of human beings in their role as physicians.

To seek help for his initial symptom, difficulty with vision,
Harry had gone first to a neighborhood optometrist. It was not
a problem of his needing new eyeglasses, and so he was passed
along from the optometrist to an ophthalmologist, then to a
specialist in internal medicine and all of the others: neurologist,
endocrinologist, radiologist, neuroradiologist. Finally, he was
seen by the neurosurgeon. A consensus of opinion was arrived
at regarding a diagnosis which should be made by any third
year medical student if he or she has been at all attentive during certain clinical courses. Harry, quite obviously, had a tumor
of his pituitary gland.

Since he had been losing sight in the outer fields of vision
of each eye for nine months, there could be no argument, seemingly, regarding the need to do something about the tumor,
now identified as pressing against the nerves controlling vision,
if in fact treatment was feasible. As his wife would reflect later
on, "Even if we had been given more time to think it over, we
would probably have agreed, eventually, to have the operation
anyway, because like everyone said, something very definitely
had to be done." Very important catch words, those. The doctors had sounded their imperative, one highly favored in the
medical community. And there is an irresistible urgency about
things which "have to be done." The problem is that there are
times when not much deliberation goes into deciding *what*.

And so the opening round in his struggle was lost by the

ordinary man whom "nobody respects," responding in lockstep with so many other unfortunates given no choice except that which "must be done." More sophisticated patients might have insisted upon a broader presentation including alternative treatment choices, as well as the reasons for having an operation, but probably they would not have been extended much respect, either. If, as commonly occurs, the various kinds of treatment are not fully or appropriately described, doctors who pass on such limited information will encounter little resistance to their final urgings from any kind of patient, howsoever endowed. In a way, the ordinary man fares the better. At least he isn't overwhelmed and made anxious by limited or flawed medical representations, meaningless deliberations, and uninformed family conferences. He has few, if any, lingering doubts and hesitations. Hence, during the time before his surgery, Harry was untroubled. The neurosurgeon's interpretation and pronouncement of his needs became just another article of Harry's simple kind of faith. If it were to happen that there would be no real further life for him after the operation, well, Harry was the kind of man to be counted on as accepting.

In the hours between his doctor's arbitrary insistence to operate and the surgery destined to obliterate his unique self, Harry did manage a brief respite into which he compressed both some of the obligation and the pleasure of being alive. Although the neurosurgeon wanted him hospitalized at once, Harry had stronger needs than his medical ones. He insisted upon having a few hours to himself until the following day. There was his ninety-year-old mother to be comforted. "I'm going to be blind if I don't have this operation. But there's not anything to worry about. We've got the very best docs in the world." That said, he had one more night to spend entwined with his new wife. There was nothing tentative about Harry on that last day.

In the morning, his wife drove him to the train on which he would proceed to the hospital and hurried off to her place of employment. On an exceptionally frigid winter's day, they went their separate ways. There would be no more embraces, flattery, consolations, reassurances, passed between them under warm covers. Now they were controlled by the kind of fate few anticipate, that of rude surprise.

And after the surgery? Should you not be told your husband is in a coma? When so many young interns and residents are consulting one another about the possible meaning of those fixed, dilated, pupils and his failure to wake up, when they have been studying the obvious midbrain hemorrhage revealed by the emergency CAT scans, should you not be told, straightforwardly, that something has gone terribly wrong and that there is grave concern for his survival? Is it in the spirit of "consecratio medici," the healing way, to send a fearful woman homeward into the night, alone, with no more solace than that the hospital would "stay in touch"? That he was being "slow to come out of anaesthesia" was hardly a meaningful kind of confidence. To tell her that was even condescending, arrogant. For Harry's wife was a sensible woman.

And where was the neurosurgeon?He had disappeared. A senior doctor in training, the neurosurgical resident, was her only source of information. It was he, who after his late night dinner and clinical rounds, telephoned to say that Harry's vital signs were normal, his heart was strong, and there appeared to be no immediate threat to his life. What did all of that mean to a woman who wanted her husband back? As days passed, various messages were passed along to her from the neurosurgeon who had operated, and always to the effect that "progress was being made." The neurosurgeon, in fact, was impatiently awaiting his earliest opportunity to send Harry on to an extended care facility. The presence of a post operative patient in such awful condition could hardly stand to enhance his professional reputation.

She was told little more. Hers was to be an evolving awareness, arrived at almost wordlessly, to the effect that Harry's immediate medical outlook was uncertain. There was encouraged a tacit understanding that any progress, should it occur, would be slow, "very slow," and no one could really predict just how things might eventually turn out. The brain, this kind of surgery, the obscure nature of any individual patient's response to operation, were all very complicated matters, and you can't always find out why these unfortunate things do happen. As for Harry's future? Suddenly, like everything else ... "It was in the hands of the Almighty." Could this be the same neurosurgeon who before surgery had given such strong insistence regarding the safety and the nicety of the impending operative procedure, so long as it was performed by his experienced hands?

As for the fact that the CAT scans, which by then had been repeated several times, all showed bleeding into the midbrain, and that the neurosurgeon had omitted from his operation certain essential and routine safeguards, or that the operation had been neither urgently required, nor the only feasible kind of treatment available for Harry's condition... those would be matters for her to discover on her own.

Why such a rush to operate? Every doctor to examine Harry had found no more than a chronic kind of pallor in one optic nerve and in spite of the longstanding nature of his illness, he could still see quite well with that very eye, and just about normally so with the other one. Even the field, i.e. the range of his vision, was but minimally restricted. Given the general medical understanding that this type of tumor grows extremely slowly, usually taking years before it becomes large enough to compress the optic fibers, it was curious that anyone should urge an immediate decision regarding any kind of treatment, much less a surgical procedure. This is particularly the case because it can happen that a patient may do poorly, however treated, if under the emotional stress brought about by precipitous intervention. Such adverse reactions are notably encountered with hasty surgery. What is called for, rather, is calm and reassurance. The patient should be brought to understand that pituitary tumors grow slowly, generally taking years to progress, and only very rarely do they compress other parts of the brain apart from the visual apparatus.

Harry and his wife should not have had to leave the neurosurgeon's office under dire warning of every conceivable problem that might occur, including the threat of a serious deterioration of various critical brain centers, should the tumor not be removed immediately. The fact that visual impairment had existed for at least nine months proved a slow kind of growth. The tumor had surely existed for years without producing any symptoms at all, but quite recently its continued enlargement had brought it into contact with the optic chiasm, a structure which joins the two optic nerves and which permits the innermost fibers of each nerve to cross to the opposite side of the brain. Pressure at this particular point had finally brought on the signs of the tumor's presence. But for that to happen the tumor had needed to expand no more than a millimeter or two during the prior several months. Even then, the body usually tolerates pressure upon nerve tissue quite well if it develops slowly over a very long time. So all that Harry really required was to know that his outlook was favorable, and that whatever treatment he might eventually choose in order to reduce the size of his pituitary tumor, recovery was to be anticipated, barring the remotest chance of complications. Then, in some detail, the neurosurgeon should have described the various kinds of available treatment.

What would ordinarily happen if Harry and his wife had known their real options? Rather than get ready for hospital admission the next day they would have returned home to consider the pros and cons of various kinds of operative procedure versus the use of radiation therapy. If, in due course, they were still not able to reach a decision they would, in all likelihood, have turned elsewhere for a second opinion. They would have been well served to hear what a radiotherapist, or some other neurosurgeon, might advise regarding treatment. There was but one risk if time were to be spent this way. It was that their particular neurosurgeon might lose his patient to the care of some other doctor.

Had they consulted any competent physician specializing in radiation therapy, such management would have been offered. If they had been advised by any well informed neurological surgeon prepared to speak forthrightly, they would have been told that radiation therapy could be expected to reverse his minimal visual handicap. It is known to do so in more than eighty per cent of patients like Harry, making surgery generally unnecessary. Surgery can be safely reserved for those patients who do not respond satisfactorily to radiation therapy. These are facts which were established in the medical literature more than forty years ago, and are based upon results obtained with thousands of patients at major medical centers. The benefits of radiation treatment do require several months to materialize, but the risk that vision will deteriorate temporarily over that interval of time is no greater than the significant chance of serious visual and other side effects occurring permanently as complications of operation. To minimize the risks of radiation therapy it is only necessary that the vision of the patient be assessed regularly and attentively by an ophthalmologist during the course of radiation treatment.

Harry was advised quite differently. His neurosurgeon told him that radiation therapy is an old-fashioned method, and that it is no longer given as primary treatment. That what was essential was a fast result before the tumor could grow any larger. He insisted that by the time any effects of radiation could take hold, his vision would be much worse. Radiation therapy, in that doctor's opinion, was merely an option that might be exercised after the operation, for an effect on parts of the tumor that could not be removed, or that might grow back some time in the future. Surgery was required and there was an urgent need to perform it during those next few days.

Is it the case that Harry would really have been treated differently had he managed to consult some other neurosurgeon? Not likely. Other neurosurgeons would probably have given him more time to decide, and would not be apt to label his condition "an emergency," but they would have recommended that same operation. After all, it was the one that happened to be *en vogue*.

However desirable it may be for patients with various neurological conditions, including that of tumor of the pituitary gland, to receive non-surgical treatment, they are not usually going to get that sort of advisement from a neurosurgeon. First off, there are few such doctors both responsible and knowledgeable enough to give them the appropriate advice. There is also the problem that surgeons have a considerable personal stake in the performance of operations. The surgical fee, all too often, is an irresistible inducement. Moreover, the technical aspects of an operative procedure have their way of providing an exciting or interesting challenge. Some insecure surgeons actually need to prove themselves in this way continuously, in which case if an appropriate opportunity to do so does not present itself, they may create one. Also, as newer or more difficult operative techniques evolve, surgeons are tempted to have a go at them, even when a legitimate need for that particular service has not materialized. And unnecessary operations also take place because doctors think to maintain their basic surgical skills by exercising them. What else could be expected from an endeavor that is subject to no appreciable oversight regulation, and which relies almost entirely upon the good faith of its professional men and women, individuals beset by all of the usual human needs and desires?

The practice of surgery is no different from the rest of medicine. It also operates as a free market system. There should be no wonder then that where supply (physicians) is in an uncontrolled and erratic relationship to demand (patients), there can be a surplus of physicians in various specialties in many communities. This is particularly true of large cities where specialists like to congregate. What this means when it comes to surgery, is that such doctors must compete for a limited number of patients, and some of those well trained hands would also be quite idle were it not for the variable performance of surgery that is often quite unnecessary.

In spite of this, at dozens of training centers, a constant search goes on to find the patients upon whom even more young doctors can operate in order to acquire necessary surgical skills and professional qualifications. Many of these neurosurgical training centers do not even exist out of need. They are there because of a relentless abiding tradition for creating endowed chairs and professorships of neurosurgery for certain physicians who then, quite often enough for it to be alarming, do whatever is required to maintain approval of the residency training programs upon which those faculty appointments of theirs depend. That includes the further performance of unnecessary surgery. The system has a way of feeding upon itself and is self propagating.

Patients like Harry also get operated upon because they may fall under the care of neurosurgeons who are not knowledgeable regarding treatment other than surgery. Such doctors graduate, typically, from institutional programs at which medical treatment is rarely discussed during the surgical training period. There is not much possibility, then, that when those graduates take their qualifying surgical examinations, they will be asked about the medical approach to conditions they have only been taught to treat surgically.

Surgeons, on top of that, seem to have developed their own peculiar mindsets and prejudices. For example, should a surgeon suggest, perhaps in a conference with colleagues, that a nonoperative type of treatment be implemented, assuredly, commonly, eyebrows would be raised. The ranks could very well close against such challenge to the surgical credo, and real questions be entertained regarding the credentials and every other kind of legitimacy of such an impudent provocateur. Should such a guileless one be male, his very manhood might be fair game for questioning.

What happens to patients, given any set of symptoms, signs, and needs, is for the most part predetermined by such considerations. It is therefore not reasonable to speculate about what might or might not have happened should Harry have gone to a different surgeon. Harry didn't have much chance of receiving, anywhere, the treatment best suiting him.

After his operation the neurological findings could only be explained by an injury of the midbrain and the adjacent visual fibers. It is in the midbrain, the upper part of the brain stem, that the right and left oculomotor or third cranial nerves, take their origin. These nerves pass forward from that location to a position alongside the pituitary gland and pass through a channel of venous blood known as the cavernous sinus. The oculomotor nerves control elevation of the upper eyelids, narrowing of the pupils, and certain other eye movements. If the centers in the midbrain from which these nerves take their origin should be injured, one would anticipate that the affected patient would exhibit exactly the disability manifested by Harry, i.e., inability to raise the eyelids, dilated pupils, and eyes turned outward. The midbrain hemorrhage seen in the CAT scan was also associated with a great deal of swelling which is known as edema. The edema progressed to the point of causing a breakdown of nerve tissue, a condition called necrosis. This was reliable indication that nerve pathways other than those of the oculomotor nerve centers had also been injured. And there was ample clinical evidence that this was the case. The nerve tracts for movement, those which innervate muscles, the so-called "motor" ones, and those sensing position, as well as the nerve cells for maintaining consciousness, the "reticular activating system," had all been damaged. Motor pathways were compromised, not only in respect of arm and leg movements, but also those for speech function and swallowing. That's why Harry had slurred speech and problems with eating when he finally regained consciousness. Medical students are taught neuroanatomy and the technique of neurological examination so that, given such neurological findings as Harry showed after surgery, they may accurately predict the location of the sort of lesion that was affirmed so clearly in his post-operative CAT scans. The final deterioration in Harry's vision was related both to surgical injury of his optic nerve fibers during removal of the tumor as well as to the eventual regrowth of tumor tissue that was not completely excised.

Although a surgical complication of this exact type has never been reported in the medical literature, it has probably occurred. This can be suggested because thousands of such operations have been performed and because very few surgical complications are ever described or documented in medical journals. The studies reported in most scientific articles are designed to emphasize how new and effective techniques can be successfully carried out, provided that stipulated safeguards are implemented. Such articles do not disclose what happens when individual neurosurgeons, particularly those not practicing in major medical centers, perform such operations, or when the necessary and required safeguards are not employed. Moreover, it is hardly likely that any neurosurgeon would publicize a case in which his treatment has been this disastrous. Serious medical and surgical complications do sometimes get recorded in hospital records, but more often they do not. Where they surface most consistently is in courts of law and in the files of insurance companies. They receive but scant attention in the medical literature or in hospital proceedings, in spite of the fact that such discussions are supposed to be a mandatory requirement for hospital accreditation. In this instance, the complication took place because the neurosurgeon did, in fact, happen to omit a necessary safeguard. During such surgery fluoroscopic x-ray is customarily used so as to distinguish the tumor from adjacent brain tissue in order that once the surgical instruments are introduced into the tumor they probe or penetrate no further than the outer limits of the tumor. But the only way such a distinction can be reliably made is to inject air into the spinal fluid so that it may bubble up into the fluid spaces at the base of the brain. The air insinuates itself between the tumor and the brain and is revealed as a dark shadow on a fluoroscopic screen, permitting the neurosurgeon to define and to stay strictly within the confines of the tumor. In such an operative field the brain is actually that upper part of the brain stem we have referred to as the midbrain, as well as another critical structure called the hypothalamus. It was not possible for the neurosurgeon to know how close his instruments were to the midbrain or to the hypothalamus because without a separating layer of air, the tumor and those vital brain structures looked quite the same. This was the case only because he did not make the critical and obligatory injection of air.

The doctor had performed many operations of this type. He was thoroughly familiar with the requirements for doing them safely. Later, in court, when queried by opposing counsel about his failure to inject the air, he responded that in his opinion such a technique was not required for this particular patient. Not only did he know the proper method very well, he was personally acquainted with those surgeons who had pioneered this operative method and who considered that part of it to be the "sine qua non" for its safe performance. He had utilized the injection of air in the past, routinely, but he did not do so when he operated upon Harry. Why not? Simply because after a great deal of success with this kind of an operation, he had become overly confident and had taken a short cut. Perhaps he had already done so with other patients and gotten away with it, becoming even more self-assured. This time, however, the result was catastrophic.

When he or she operates, the surgeon is in command and draws pride from his skill, his judgement, his boldness, his ingenuity. He usually has the respect of other doctors and attending personnel who are present. Often the tensions and the excitement which may be generated during moments when that skill is called upon to surmount problems with hemorrhage, and to work competently under charged circumstanes, convert to a shared heroic experience for all of those present. With some surgeons that excitement is heady indeed and becomes intoxicating, addictive. It can compromise clinical judgment and induce susceptible surgeons to test uncharted waters. If they succeed, they may be emboldened to the point of harboring the delusion that howsoever a particular operation may be performed by them, in their hands it will be safe. They have become transcendent, infallible. This was such a surgeon.

But no one is infallible. And a doctor is not at liberty to attempt what is untested or to abandon accepted safeguards without permission from both the patient and the hospital. As for heroism, it is not to be found in any operating room. Heroes put their own lives at risk for someone, or something else. What kind of bravery can any surgeon lay claim to when all that's risked is the life of a completely helpless patient?

Although Harry is usually tranquil, there are certain moments, occurring every so often, when a remarkable change takes place. Without apparent provocation, his face becomes flushed, he perspires profusely, his blood pressure becomes elevated, and he lashes out indiscriminately, striking at the innocent air and unoffending objects about him, with obvious, violent rage. His face contorts and his lips are drawn back in an intimidating snarl. Then, in just a few moments, the episode is

over. When asked about these attacks, he admits to an awareness of the movements, but there is no evidence he has actually
experienced any of the strong emotions one would assume from
the display. And it could be that he is only aware of having had
the movements because afterwards, his muscles ache for days.

In 1929, Philip Bard demonstrated in experimental animals
that removal of the brain above the hypothalamus produced a
syndrome which came to be called "sham rage." The animal
could not actually experience the rage because the part of the
brain which recognizes such an emotional phenomenon had
been removed. In 1937, Stephen Ranson reported that identical
findings were to be observed in laboratory animals following
electrical stimulation of the posterior hypothalamus. The condition has never been described in man.

It was precisely these same areas of the brain through which
the neurosurgical instruments would have had to pass as they
coursed into Harry's midbrain, necessarily destroying them.
Thus, all of the post-operative symptoms and signs of this patient
can be readily and fully understood.

It is an irony that these attacks of sham rage have no counterpart by way of emotions that can actually be felt by Harry.
If anyone is entitled to real rage it is he, but what is seen by
observers of these attacks has no pertinence. They are only the
mock display of how Harry should quite rightly react and feel,
given what's been done to him, but cannot.

On the other hand, the neurosurgeon who is responsible
for Harry's pathetic condition does have feelings. He complains,
and whines, and resents bitterly the injustice of having had
charges pressed against him by the patient's wife. For him, that
very limited notoriety is nevertheless an affront to his reputation, although, as is customary, he has never been held to any
formal professional accounting by his peers.

There are two other prominent neurosurgeons who practice in his Illinois town. Why, he asks, for no better reason than
what happened to Harry, should the word be out, and they be
favored so as to draw off his referrals? He still claims to have
done nothing wrong during the operation and is adamant that
were Harry to present himself today, with the same clinical

problem, he would perform exactly the same operation, in exactly the same way. This he rants vehemently, but during his court trial he chose to settle the case against him and agreed to compensate his patient rather than risk an adverse jury verdict.

Hopefully, there are times when people, including this neurosurgeon, feel quite a bit differently than they would lead us to believe. They, at least, have that possibility. It is only Harry who has been cut off, forever, by a surgeon's instrument, from all feelings, including those we would expect him to have and to which he is fully entitled.

4

Leroy

STANDARD

A physician or hospital assuming responsibility for the treatment of a head injured patient that has been unconscious, however briefly, must see to it that the patient undergoes a CAT scan of the brain as quickly as possible, after presentation.

L eroy's pupils were last examined when the youth lay upon the mortuary table. They were observed and duly noted, along with other findings and measurements usually considered significant by a pathologist. Some unknowing observer might think those pupils had been frozen half-wide in reactive horror at the sight of his fifteen-year-old burly assailant coming on in such a rush to pummel him to the ground. But that was not the reason for this terminal kind of mid-dilatation of the pupils. Their first enlargement, occasioned by his initial fright, had subsided almost immediately. The body adrenaline, which brings on such a reaction, has only brief effect. It would be many hours later, when a blood clot within his brain had produced enormous pressure, that the subsequent, different, and finally fatal kind of pupillary change took place.

The pathologist made the customary ear to ear transverse incision of the scalp peeling it forward until it covered the face. Next, the skull cap was sawed away, neatly, leading to a slow ooze of dark blood which ebbed to a stop. The blood had exited from the right temporal lobe, breaking from the depths at a point where the brain surface, the cortex, had been lacerated during Leroy's assault and beating. For the pathologist, employed as county coroner, the appearance of that amount of blood meant no more than that he should measure it and then continue with his other systematic determinations. Yet, if just a few hours earlier that same quantity of blood had been evacuated from the brain, not in the morgue but in an operating room, everyone present would have registered relief and satisfaction to see it stream forth as the mark of a probably successful life-saving surgical procedure. But this was a morgue scene and provided no more than a macabre, rather cruel, false staging of the operation Leroy had needed but was denied.

A blood clot within the brain is called, in medical parlance, an intracerebral hematoma. When a hematoma of Leroy's type and location is diagnosed and treated in timely fashion, the victim of such an injury will usually recover. One might even imagine Leroy, having enjoyed such kindly intervention, as early as his first postoperative day, already quite ready, very much willing, and surprisingly able to plot some quick revenge against Bolo, his ultimate adversary. And that operation would have been so easy to perform! It certainly wouldn't have required the large skull opening made by the coroner. Just a single drilled hole, less than an inch across, would have turned the trick. It would not have been necessary, either, to probe to any depths in the brain to search out this clot. It needed only the provision of a way, any way, out. Just that small opening in the skull, plus a mere nick in the underlying outer membrane of the brain, the dura mater, and the brain, swollen by its reaction to the clot, would have expelled it to the surface. Then, Leroy Brown would have been a most fortunate patient in a neurosurgical intensive care unit, and not a poor black boy on a slab in the morgue of a small gulf coast town where after some high school locker room shenanigans, his young life seems not to have counted for very much.

A boy, gone at fourteen, is an incongruous sight. Lifeless children are still too verged upon their newness to be credibly, dead. We take for granted their entitlement to longevity. It is also sometimes difficult to see them seriously as patients, in the way we regard adults. This, in spite of their having the more to lose by forfeiture of life. But children have no more prospect of a return to life, or a stronger hold upon it, than the rest of us. Treatment then, if it is to be prejudiced at all, should be inclined in their favor. It is a sad fact, however, that, as in the case of Leroy, their young lives can be cast away as easily as those of their elders.

What might be surmised regarding the precise moment that Leroy's fate was sealed? Young Doctor Dominick, who was first to examine him, would time it to when those blows were delivered to his head. "It was a fatal force, and it was that alone which killed him. If you want to look for reasons that he died, blame the guy who hit him and who murdered him. Don't involve me. I did nothing wrong. All I did was try to save him."

Most matters can be made as complicated or as straightforward as one may contrive but rarely is anything medical that simple. Leroy did not die instantly when attacked, and many things happened before he passed. Deciding who was to blame for his death, and whether or not it was inevitable, requires determining if it could have been prevented. Of course, his death in legal terms allows of no such consideration. He was the victim of a crime. Under most law, the fact that he might have been saved is irrelevant. So by those criteria, Leroy died by the blow which felled him.

It is supposed to follow, therefore, that he died by the hand which delivered that blow. But was there some irresponsibility connected with his death having as much, or even more to do with its determination, than the criminally obvious events as they are known? Exploration of that possibility privileges the contention that Leroy's dying was no more fairly attributable to Bolo, who in his frenzy flailed out only in the general direction of Leroy's body, having no idea at all of a destructive best focus for his attack, than to Leroy himself, for initiating an entire year of provocation by his relentless taunting of Bolo as an ethnic outsider in his school.

The so-called killer, as well as the killed, were really innocents. What finally determined Leroy's death, what set the point in time when his course became irreversible, had more to do with what did not happen to him than with what did.

A good first step in the search for causes is to totally ignore Doctor Dominick's admonition. And, when finally all is known, one might ask if Leroy's fatal countdown didn't actually commence precisely when this doctor completed his training in emergency medicine. It was then that he assumed responsibility for the care of head-injured patients not having comprehended the basic principles governing the management of such patients.

Whatever the depth of a doctor's familiarity with various treatment options, there usually operates an awareness of certain illnesses and injuries about which he or she is uninformed to the point of feeling at least uneasily uncertain, if not agonizingly ignorant, regarding management. So unlike Harry's doctor, who was well versed in his chosen field, and who knew what he had to know and should have done better, Doctor Dominick carried on in his emergency room duties, including the care of patients with head injury, probably knowing full well that he was exceeding his capabilities, yet not having an inclination to do something about it. One can reasonably anticipate that such a physician would inevitably render poor care for lack of knowing what was required. As for his conscience in such matters, it was that fundamental absence which permitted him to continue practicing emergency medicine in the way that he did.

But would he not at least seek consultation, call in someone else, a neurosurgeon for example? This he did, and often, but only when the requirements for neurosurgery were obvious, as when patients were admitted with depressed skull fractures or were completely unconscious and had a widely dilated nonreactive pupil. The problem is that when patients did not have these obvious conditions, but did require competent assessment, Doctor Dominick, although not knowing how to go about something like that, could not afford the embarrassment of seeming to need a neurosurgeon to examine every patient with head injury coming to his emergency room. He was canny enough, however, to understand that the odds were in favor of his not being found out. He could continue to be uninformed because most patients who are briefly unconscious after head injury eventually make uncomplicated recoveries without any particular treatment. This much he had learned by simple observation. He also appreciated that should things not turn out quite that well because of a failure on his part to make the necessary clinical distinctions regarding various complications stemming from head injury, there would be no penalty for him because bad results in such patients are commonly taken for granted and may not even be detected, much less investigated. Even when they are, no one is apt to draw medical blame. The typical and usually favored summation for such an unlikely inquiry, if it should take place, is that "death was unavoidable and unrelated to treatment." So it was that Doctor Dominick came to chance it with Leroy's life. The odds were in favor of his getting away with it. As it happened, luck ran out for both of them, but the price was paid only by Leroy. Taken to court for his malpractice, Doctor Dominick agreed to a settlement. Whereupon he returned to his clinical practice in the same emergency room as a physician in good standing. There is meager consolation or plausible reassurance to be drawn from declarations by his lawyer that "Dominick has learned a lot about head injury from all of this."

But doesn't everyone take chances? Is that not a special human attribute and one of our most persistent inclinations? When everything has been considered, allowed for, and even when it can't be so, do we not experiment by moving on anyway, and ultimately tempting fate, by taking a chance? Humans are stubbornly, unaccountably, perhaps even instinctively, optimistic about assuming risk. The disposition to gamble may even be at the core of our evolutionary pressure. Certainly, it is hardly likely that our sometimes natural enthusiasm for abandoning caution can be suppressed. But what happens when this inclination to tempt fate undermines or substitutes for responsible labor, for no better reason than that it is so much easier to just lay back, abstain from being diligent, and take a chance? What happens should one fall into the hands of such an emergency room physician?

Doctors like this one, apparently born to inaction, quick only to chance at doing nothing, hardly consider their diagnostic or therapeutic alternatives. They are happy with their inertia. They find contentment in lazy irresponsibility, an option entrenched by the reinforcement of pleasant, successful experience with such dangerous ways. Nor will a choice for dedicated effort in the interest of someone else be made by constitutionally lethargic doctors, when after years of study they suddenly realize they can stop pounding the books. It has dawned upon them that patients do get better on their own and that the risk of their professional inadequacy being detected can be safely taken. It is unfortunate that by then they may very well have been officially certified as not only qualified, but also trustworthy.

In spite of newspaper accounts of medical malpractice, we still seem to like and to trust our doctors. At least that is what people say when they are polled. The relationship to one's doctor, however, is based entirely upon trust. It is generally assumed by patients that the physician has only one purpose, to be of service. The doctor is supposed to ask, "How can I help you?." And then a vulnerable individual recounts a medical history, placing his or her life under the discretionary control of another human being. If the doctor is surrounded by ostentatious evidence of material wealth, if he projects an unbounded ego, or even if he is barely communicative, those signs, which might raise questions in any other relationship, are not permitted consideration in this one. They must not, if it is to work. And even if theirs seems to be a contract based upon the briefest of interviews, or the most spotty of all possible examinations, such suspicions must not intrude. To be a proper patient, for there to be a sound, secure, patient-to-doctor relationship, the patient must become the ideal, unquestioning, potential victim. Is there another association of individuals, not bound by blood ties, so peculiar?

Public concern over the practice of medicine has increased in recent years, but that apprehension has been largely about the occasionally deviant physician. There is little inclination to accept the suggestion that the problem is more prevalent to the point of being innate; that doctors are all too often not deserving of trust.

Because the death of Leroy was the result of such a professional failure, that of a misplaced trust, and is unacceptable, it would be well before examining his death more closely, to perhaps anticipate it in the light of seemingly minor but yet widespread, deliberate acts of irresponsibility and ignorant persistence well typified by commonplace instances of unacceptable medical behavior.

Careful observation can confirm that in as ordinary an act as the drawing of blood for almost any purpose, physicians often break with the requirements of sterile technique. The skin may not be wiped clean with an antiseptic. The needle may be brought carelessly into contact with the doctor's own hand, or be unsteriled when removed from its packaging, and then be used anyway. A scrutiny of the daily events in an operating room will reveal the occasional surgeon at a scrub sink cutting short on the amount of time necessary to cleanse his hands and forearms. He is hurrying to get on with his case load. Perhaps, just as an assistant surgeon completes his own surgical scrub, that doctor, in turn, makes elbow contact with the soap dispenser, or some other nonsterile object; but instead of repeating the scrubbing procedure, goes on to enter the operating room and participate in the surgery. He believes that his hands, by their very nature, are cleaner and harbor fewer bacteria than the next fellow's. Another example: a surgeon with torn glove continues to operate upon a patient, knowing full well that his hand is no longer sterile but not wanting to stop for the few moments required for a glove change. A different surgeon looks across the room and notices that a nurse is resting, seated on a stool, her surgical gown open at the back and making contaminating contact with the surgical instrument tray. He says nothing. Our observation continues. Occasionally a surgical nose is seen, no longer covered because the operating mask has been allowed to slip down, or the eyes of a surgeon peering over his mask have occasion to detect an anesthesiologist not wearing any mask at all, and in the act, as well, of moving nonsterile equipment too close to the surgical field. No action is taken. No words are spoken. A doctor perspires and drips directly into the surgical wound. He considers his sweat to be innocuous. It is different from the sweat of a doctor who stops if he drips, requests a sweat band, and then floods the operative field with antibiotic solutions. Or, he considers that his sweat is of the lucky kind, and can be chanced to be non-threatening to the patient. His hair is also charmed and may safely dangle free from beneath his operating head gear. "Careless" is the right word for it. But how much less of this kind of caring can some patients endure?

Ask about these things and you will be told they are of no consequence. Accept, if you are gullible, that most of such precautions regarding sterility are superfluous and not really necessary. It appears easier for some physicians to contrive false reassurances than to change irresponsible behavior. If patients were not generally quite tough and resistant to infection, it would not usually require more than one oversight like these to injure them. Fortunately, patients can be that hardy. Those who are not, don't make out so well. They become infected. Some suffer the effects of bacteria in the blood stream. Others have infections localized to their surgical wounds or in remote organs. Patients can and do die from such infections. All too often they are fancified by being designated "iatrogenic." These and other kinds of everyday medical deviation are not only matters of potential injury but it could be said, of deadly mayhem just waiting to happen. In the case of Leroy, one of them became actual.

When a son has been rushed to the hospital by ambulance, and a teen-aged daughter has taken the family car to school, it is not easy for a working mother to reach her son's side quickly in rural America. What one must do is call the daughter's principal and get permission for her to leave school so as to transport you. Where Leroy's mother did her housecleaning there was no street outside into which she might rush and hail down a cruising taxi. And so she waited patiently, as many people have learned to wait, abidingly and numbly, during the most trying of life's crises. They have no real option to do otherwise. Thus she waited while at her daughter's school the word was passed along through prescribed channels until finally the daughter was granted permission to depart. It was not to profit Leroy or his family one bit that this awkward sort of communal behavior was finally mobilized in his behalf. It took the better part of two hours for his mother to reach his side. By then, in his own turn, he'd already been subjected to other efforts, similarly well systematized. In the long run, they wouldn't matter either. Doctor Dominick would see to that.

At Leroy's school, once told of his unconscious state by the gym teacher, the principal had summoned an ambulance. Upon their arrival in the gymnasium locker room the ambulance technicians applied a cervical collar, determined Leroy's blood pressure and pulse, placed him on a fracture board, and in less than ten minutes time had him before the admitting nurse in the local hospital emergency room. They gave her the history of his having been unconscious for several minutes following the beating. The nurse dutifully entered this information into the record, conducted her own examination, and repeated the measurement of Leroy's blood pressure and pulse. So far everything was being done compliantly according to well planned protocols and insistences. School principals, secretaries, gym teacher, ambulance technicians and the emergency room nurse, as well as Leroy's mother and sister who were out there somewhere doing what was required to get them to the hospital, each and every one of them meeting their obligations on his behalf. How could Leroy go wrong? Especially since at that point in time he was fully conscious, beginning to wonder what had happened to him, and what was going on.

For things to go wrong required only the appearance of Doctor Dominick. Not that anyone could ever charge him with inability to make quick decisions. Snap judgments were his forté. Within minutes of this doctor's encounter of Leroy, the boy was summarily discharged from the hospital. The paper trail left by Doctor Dominick contains some astonishing entries. Inscribed by his hand, and penned with style and grand flourish, was a notation that Leroy had no idea of how he'd been injured, or how he'd come to be a patient in this emergency room. The doctor's diagnosis was head trauma, cerebral concussion. The treatment was discharge to the custody of his mother with special instructions. His commentary in the medical record also referred to certain observations by the ambulance technicians to the effect that Leroy, according to witnesses, having been struck in the face, had fallen rearward, hitting the back of his head, first against a steel locker door, and then upon a concrete floor. His most remarkable written entry was the opinion that Leroy had sustained no loss of consciousness. That conclusion was inscribed directly below the nursing notation of a "history of loss of consciousness" and above his own observation that Leroy couldn't remember anything, which of itself, by every commonplace medical acceptance, meant that necessarily a significant disturbance of consciousness had taken place. Close by, in the hospital record, a mere two lines away from Doctor Dominick's note, a nurse had also entered the worrisome finding of an elevated blood pressure. Elevated blood pressure is usually associated with intracranial bleeding. Doctor Dominick does not read nursing notes. He believes they are written by nurses, to be read by nurses. They are something for the continuity of nursing care and not of any particular medical value or for the edification of doctors needing to monitor their patients. He also does not read medical books, or he would know what most fight fans either understand or suspect. The fellow not able to tell what's happened to him has surely, at least to some degree, been knocked out. And if that fellow hasn't a clue as to what he was doing before his injury, or what transpired after he woke up, then the period of altered consciousness was more than brief, and the blow was apt to have been a severe one. These considerations, which relate to the duration of such periods of retrograde amnesia and of post injury confusion, are the basic stuff of neurology text books. It is also basic that such patients are not sent away from the hospital. They are retained for close observation and monitoring. They have CAT scans performed upon them to see if there has been any intracranial bleeding.

Doctor Dominick, turning a quick heel in another direction, his white coat fluttering behind him, was not off to bone up on head injury in books dealing with neurology. Nor was he to tarry in the emergency room and finger through the pages of a manual dealing with the management of head trauma, a required reading for doctors who work in the emergency rooms of accredited hospitals. Where he might have been headed is not important. That he was empty headed, at least on the subject of brain injury, and intent on gambling with Leroy's well being, is surely so.

Leroy's mother and sister arrived at the hospital anxious and breathless, only to be told Leroy was doing just fine and was ready to go home. Under such circumstances one would expect, as a matter of ordinary courtesy and decency, much less professional responsibility, that some doctor would sit them down and explain his assessment and recommendations. Instead, what they got was a piece of paper, impersonally slipped to them through the pass window of the waiting room, listing what was to be looked for, after they were home, in the event that his condition deteriorated.

Leroy was slumped over to one side with his head rolled backwards as an orderly pushed his wheelchair towards the exit and away from the special care he needed. Trailing behind him, Leroy's sister read to her mother what for both of them amounted to a cryptic advisory. "It say here, Mama, that if we can't wake him up, or if he vomits a lot, we gotta call the doctor. Who that gonna be, Mama?" There was no suggestion that it should be a doctor at this same hospital. Nor was there any warning about headache, which could be an early symptom of pending trouble long before the appearance of more serious signs or complaints.

With the orderly's help, Leroy was placed on the back seat of the car, where he reclined almost at once, looking vacant and unable to answer questions put to him by either his sister or his mother regarding what had happened in the high school locker room. But they had no recourse other than to set out once more, in what was a sort of reverse playback of their earlier transit to the hospital, with notable exceptions. Reverse movie or video playbacks are at an accelerated speed, having often an amusing air to them. Here, the subjects moved painfully slow and sad-eyed. Also, Leroy was in no condition to reverse himself all the way back to his school.

For that reason he was left in the custody of concerned grandparents who were cautioned to watch him closely, whereupon Leroy's sister drove her mother back to where she worked and then went on, once again, to her own school.

Hardly had Leroy's mother started up her vacuum cleaner when she was summoned to her employer's phone. It had become almost impossible to arouse Leroy. When his grandparents were able to do so, he made no sense and was vomiting repeatedly where he lay in his grandmother's bed. Not knowing any doctor to summon, the mother, now very frightened, called back to the hospital. Her call was taken by the same nurse who had made out Leroy's discharge papers. "I think you had best bring him back" said she, with no hint of urgency. What Leroy needed right then was an ambulance, and he needed it desperately soon. He was starting to slip away. But how was his mother to know she was being misled, that she had to move more quickly? After all, didn't children sometimes vomit, or become drowsy, for any number of reasons?

She called her daughter's principal once more so that she might leave school with their car. After the young girl picked her up, they drove to the grandparents' house and by the efforts of four straining people, Leroy was placed again across the rear seat where he collapsed and slept. Then, in that pathetic fashion, they were on their way anew to the hospital. Could this really be happening in present day America? Was this what we call our modern medicine?

When they finally arrived at the emergency room, a new admission record and a new hospital chart were made out. Everything was repeated again quite deliberately and efficiently for the boy who slept. The nurse neatly penned her commentary that Leroy was back for "reevaluation," having been seen there some four hours earlier. The elevated blood pressure was even higher and it was duly noted. But now there was also a very slow pulse. These were obvious indications, important diagnostic signs, of increased intracranial pressure. When pressure rises within the cranial cavity, blood in the arterial circulation becomes impeded in its flow through the arteries of the brain. This reduction of blood flow creates the potentially brain damaging condition called cerebral ischemia. Blood pressure then usually rises reflexly, automatically, in an effort to counter the heightening pressure within the cranial cavity, against which the flow of blood, based upon its own pressure, must somehow manage to work. Such balancing of pressures through elevation of blood pressure is called the Cushing reflex. A slow pulse often goes along with this kind of response. Leroy's brain, adjacent to the blood clot which had developed within his temporal lobe, was beginning to swell and was causing the elevation of intracranial pressure.

Doctor Dominick reappeared to evaluate Leroy. Again, he failed to note the abnormally high blood pressure, or to detect how much the pulse had slowed, the condition of "bradycardia." Instead of making those relevant, important observations, he stated in the record that his clinical assessment was being handicapped by the patient's inability to cooperate. Leroy would not follow commands. He inclined either to do nothing or to merely squirm when bothered. Doctor Dominick had no recollection of lessons received in early training when emphasis was placed upon essential but relatively simple techniques customarily used for the evaluation of unconscious or uncooperative patients. Also, he confessed to the record that he was unable to visualize with his ophthalmoscope the patient's eyegrounds.

If only he had managed to master that simple skill, he would have probably observed within Leroy's eyes distended retinal veins no longer possessing their normal pulsations. In all likelihood he would also have seen that the optic nerve heads, the optic "discs," were beginning to swell. These are further diagnostic signs of increased intracranial pressure. That Leroy was lethargic was all he ascertained. Doctor Dominick's other contribution, as entered in the record where space was provided for diagnosis, consisted not of diagnosis at all but of commentary: "reevaluation for head injury." On the order sheet he wrote "CAT scan of head." Then, once again, he walked away.

Television foists upon us much over-blown endless scenarios, theatrically exaggerated and distorted, wherein family members, rescue squads, emergency technicians, doctors and nurses, all giving wondrous displays of proficient teamwork, go on, like as not, to triumph by their salvage of some lucky injured patient. Coupled with the display of new technology, these are awesome spectacles indeed! And that's what people expect to happen. But it is not how such events usually play out in the real world. One may safely ignore the TV commercials run by hospitals or insurance companies vying for new business and new subscribers. Not only do those who race about in ambulances and helicopters commonly bungle their jobs, but in emergency rooms as well, all too often, there is incompetence. Doctors and nurses can be poorly informed and accustomed to do no more than make the required entries into medical charts, having little idea of either the meaning or the purpose of all their compulsory charting. They may also fail to know when consultation is needed, or when to take advantage of all the new technology at their command.

In this emergency room it is improbable that Doctor Dominick or the nurses even properly understood the real purpose to be served by that customary slip of paper handed to Leroy's mother when he was sent away a few hours earlier. It is supposed to be something that family members can refer to in circumstances of head injury not associated with loss of consciousness, or when x-rays are negative, so that in the unlikely event of delayed bleeding into the brain or cranial cavity, early symptoms may be caught soon enough for a patient to be brought back to the hospital promptly. Not only did the medical personnel not realize that Leroy needed to be kept in the hospital so that special studies could be done immediately, but to their thinking the so called "head slip" handed to his mother was simply for their own self protection. As long as it could be established that his relatives had had some kind of formal warning, it could be argued later, if things took a turn for the worse or even for the harsh inevitable, that the family simply did not follow instructions. Hospitals and their employees are protected like this while being paid for little more than diligent entries into charts, punched time clocks, and adherence to a set protocol. They are not under any obligation, however, by any operating standard of care, to function with appropriate expertise in the management of specific medical or surgical conditions.

It is generally assumed by those who do know something about Leroy's kind of situation, that if a patient has suffered brief loss of consciousness following a head injury, that is, a concussion, enough force has probably been directed to the skull to be at least potentially capable of producing injury more serious than that of the simple concussion. A skull fracture may have occurred, or a hemorrhage, and the bleeding can be either into the brain substance or between the brain and skull in relationship to a fibrous membrane called the dura. Such bleeding is intracerebral, subdural, or extradural in location. Bleeding as a secondary effect of head injury can develop immediately or after a delay, and may or may not betray its presence by causing symptoms or physical signs depending upon its location and how quickly or slowly the blood accumulates.

Because of these considerations, in cases of concussion, patients are not supposed to be sent away from the hospital. Rather, they are held for observation, and CAT scans are performed before they are ever released. Such patients are detained for at least 24 to 48 hours to assure that none of these serious conditions are evolving. The most prudent physicians will perform CAT scans both on admission and once again before discharge of the patient, because delayed bleeding that is initially asymptomatic may take place after a scan done at the time of admission has been negative. If clots are discovered, and are associated with significant evidence of pressure, they must be removed surgically. Skull x-rays should also be carried out in order to ascertain the presence of a fracture. Fractures, if of a depressed variety, compress the brain and have to be surgically elevated promptly in order to reduce the risk of such patients becoming epileptic in the future. When fractures cross certain vascular channels of the skull containing important blood vessels, there is an increased possibility of bleeding and other complications requiring especially attentive surveillance and treatment. If those persons working in the emergency room on the day of Leroy's first appearance had been knowledgeable about such things, Leroy would have been kept in the hospital, evaluated, and saved by an operation.

Leroy has a place now only in the memory of family and friends. If one were to regard his hospital chart as the historical account of his passing, and explore it of a mind to determine precisely how that life was lived at its end, difficulties would be encountered. Is it not odd that one should have as good an idea of the last moments of Caesar as those of Leroy, who because he was critically ill in a modern hospital, was supposed to have had every aspect and significant change of his condition recorded? Doctor Dominick never managed to describe his patient's physical condition at all. In fact, he made a point of writing in the hospital chart that such detailed observation was not possible. It was supposedly hampered by Leroy's inability to respond. Pity the poor patient, who for being stuporous or agitated, does not cooperate sufficiently to reveal himself! To the extent he detected anything at all about Leroy other than his lethargy, there is not a single clue. Even if he had acknowledged what appeared to be normal about Leroy, or if he had described some pertinent negative findings, like the absence of a stiff neck, or abnormal reflexes, there would exist at least the conventional perceptions to which a reader of records is entitled. Society, after all, has had a hand in making it possible for people like Doctor Dominick to get a medical education, and by that investment of its resources has the right to be assured that hospital records are properly recorded and maintained. But this doctor recorded only what he considered to be the "pertinent positive findings." So in the place where a physician is expected to enter those clinical observations that may be read sometime later, and which would render a precise, detailed description of Leroy's last conscious moments, enabling any subsequent examiner to understand what had transpired, there is only blank lined paper.

"What's your problem? Everybody understands it's the way I do things!" was his protest when called upon later, in court, to explain. Unfortunately, nothing had ever been done about it. Doctor Dominick had been going his own way, his bad habits accumulating undetected, for a long time. He had more important callings than to fill up pages with clinical observations of no importance to him. Not for a moment did he ever consider they might be quite significant to someone else, someone having to provide after care to his patients, and happening to know more than he did. As for those things of greater importance needing his attention on that particular day, the superseding emergencies claimed by him of "patients with stroke, heart attack, fractures, burns, bullet wounds, pneumonia, GI bleeds and what not, you name it!," Leroy was his only patient in that emergency room, contrary to all of the later testimony of Doctor Dominick.

Doctor Dominick had written an order for a CAT scan. He did not specify when he wanted it to be performed. He would have it that since everybody "knew how he did things," it should have been carried out immediately, as an emergency. "All of my CAT scans are emergencies!" That is what he insisted, when questioned as to why there was a respectable delay in getting it done. But, in fact, his request for the scan was sent to the x-ray department as he had ordered it, as a matter of routine, so that is precisely how the x-ray technician felt obliged to respond. It would be performed, whenever convenient, later in the day. If a doctor really wants a test or a procedure to be done right away, he writes "STAT" alongside his written order. Then it will be carried out immediately, unless there is a conflict with some other emergency competing for the time, the personnel, or the equipment. In court, Dominick wasn't able to give a precise reason for his ordering of the CAT scan, much less one for wanting it to be done as an emergency. He didn't even communicate a meaningful diagnosis to the radiologist. On the x-ray requisition form he had written "post concussion syndrome." Only persons suffering from headaches, dizziness, or problems with sleep, concentration, memory, appetite, tremors, long after a head injury, may have that disorder. The term does not apply to drowsy patients who are vomiting, have elevated blood pressure and slow pulse, short hours after sustaining a blow to the head.

What more might Leroy have done to attract the attention of his doctor? He had come back to the emergency room a second time. That alone should have sufficed, but it seems not to have done so. Secluded in an alcove with curtains drawn about him, how was he even to be under effective "observation"? And so, in short order, he became restless, moaned, and started again to vomit, but now frequently and forcefully. Vomiting of that sort is called projectile, and is a further sign of increased intracranial pressure. But a doctor cannot respond to the signs of cerebral irritability or of pressure unless he knows them and sees them. Leroy persisted at it. He thrashed about, his movements becoming violent and nonpurposeful. Nurses, fearing for his safety, tied him down. They secured him to his stretcher bed with wrist and ankle restraints. His blood pressure, already elevated, rose higher. And his heart rate also slowed further as certain parts of the brain stem, their blood flow compromised by the mounting pressure, fired off impulses which descended along a nerve called the vagus to retard his heart rhythm. Soon he became quiet, lapsing into a stupor. It was then that the nurses first recorded a moderate enlargement of his right pupil.

If, for any reason, one side of the brain begins to swell, its expansion carries it toward the middle of the cranial cavity. It cannot push outwardly because of containment by the hard bones of the skull. Such directional shift of the brain is always an ominous occurrence. That is so because the middle of the cranial cavity is occupied by the brain stem, through which nerve impulses for sensations must ascend on their way to higher brain centers, and through which impulses for the direction of movement also pass, but downward from upper levels to the various muscles of the limbs and trunk. The brain stem is also the control center for vital functions such as consciousness, blood pressure regulation and respiration, as well as the various cranial nerves connecting to the eyes, face, ears, mouth, throat, chest and abdomen. If there should be a severe enough movement of one side of the brain toward the middle of the cranial cavity, it will cause major symptoms and signs by the pressure it exerts against the strategically centered brain stem and also the third cranial nerve which controls the size of the pupil. Because it is the inner aspect of the swollen brain which actually compresses this portion of the brain stem known as the midbrain, and because that swollen part happens to be the "uncus" of the temporal lobe, the resulting clinical syndrome is called an "uncal herniation." The patient becomes less responsive, manifesting various degrees of paralysis, in association with enlargement of the pupil. It is a condition representing a major clinical emergency. Often, it is the abnormally dilated pupil which gives the first indication of life being so threatened. Treatment must be started quickly before both pupils become widely dilated and the patient is comatose.

There once lived a neurosurgeon, now long passed, by the name of Haddington, who would probably condone Doctor Dominick's way of handling his patient. It was Doctor Haddington's habit to attend most of the neurosurgical conferences in his part of the country, at which, during private discussions, but not ever in open conference, he would gratuitously confide to shocked listeners his irrevocable conviction that neurosurgical emergencies simply did not exist. He would exult over this, his special oddball notion, to which he seemed exclusively privy, and be all the more infuriating because of the ridicule he inclined to heap on so much of what he'd borne witness to during his long years of practice and which he considered to be so much misguided neurosurgical rushing about in a predictably futile effort to save lives. With eyes twinkling in self delight, and a flick of hand to signal rebuttal not possible, he'd bring cigarette holder to mouth, light up, spew clouds of smoke above the heads of those around him, and await the inevitable outraged response. But there would be no further comment from him, just a smug conceitful smile, indicting everyone else for their damned galvanized to action, persistent, foolishness. Ring that fellow up any hour of the night, and always, "It can hold until morning." Never would he even interrupt his office hours, change his hospital schedule, or leave one patient, in order to save another. To his thinking, if surgical interventions were to be beneficial, it depended upon skill, never upon timing. Doctor Haddington and Doctor Dominick would be the perfect pair. They might even be fancifully imagined as having a splendid time together. Perhaps one can see them strolling along a hospital corridor, moving away from the emergency room in which Leroy grows steadily worse. Affably they amble towards the cafeteria for lunch, exchanging pleasantries in passing with colleagues of the medical staff, their minds on other matters. Or, if they should be imagined rather as now they really are, there would be the older one rolling not the least bit in his dark place, and Doctor Dominick troubled not one whit, either, for what has been brought down upon Leroy and other patients like him.

It happened, almost three hours later, that there was a change of nursing shift and an observant nursing supervisor became alarmed by Leroy's appearance. She had seen patients in the past diagnosed to have uncal herniation. To her, a dilated pupil meant a serious situation. Something finally clicked at last with Doctor Dominick also when this astute nurse summoned him back to examine Leroy and confronted him, as well, with the elevated blood pressure and slow pulse which he'd been ignoring. Barely had Doctor Dominick commenced his reevaluation of Leroy but that he no longer responded at all, becoming rigid, stiffening his limbs, and arching his back—the state of decerebrate rigidity from pressure of the uncus against the brain stem. In just a few more moments, the pupil which had enlarged earlier became widely dilated and no longer reacted to light. Leroy's respirations were becoming irregular and shallow.

Doctor Dominick suddenly came alive and rushed about in a virtual frenzy. "Why is this patient still here? How come he hasn't had the CAT scan I ordered? What the hell is going on?" Everyone else was immediately to blame. What other way for him to start taking cover? But if now he was frantic, it was the result, even then, of still having no idea of what was called for. Leroy needed intravenous mannitol, a drug for reducing intracranial pressure. He required an endotracheal tube through which to breathe and to be connected to a respirator. These things should have been done right away. Leroy had no need, instead, for Doctor Dominick to yank at the bed sheet upon which he lay, and to be jerked across to another stretcher, but that's what happened. Then off down the hall he was jostled and hurtled to the x-ray scanning room, Doctor Dominick straining at the head of the stretcher, two nurses pushing from behind. Once there they came upon a startled x-ray technician who was persuaded to remove another not too ill patient from the machine, so that Leroy could be studied in his stead. The problem, which no one recognized, would not be the simple mechanics of getting him into the scanner, but what he might be like when eventually they'd pull him out, if nothing else was done for him right then and there.

By now, it was six hours past the optimal time for getting the CAT scan, and with Leroy in rapidly deteriorating condition, Doctor Dominick was still going about everything in the wrong way. If this was how emergencies were to be managed, then Doctor Haddington was probably correct, and a doctor might just as well stay home in bed and ignore desperately sick patients, patients who otherwise treated might have a good chance of survival and recovery. Handle them by Doctor Dominick's method and they will surely die. Haddington's ghost could affirm, were it spectator to this scene, that it was exactly in that same fashion he had himself responded to acute neurosurgical situations when he had first started out as a well-intentioned young doctor, but knowing no better than Dominick. Over his early years, therefore, he had accumulated, not wisdom, but the terrible results of his many clinical blunders. No wonder, then, that he gave up finally on the prospects of being useful by means of "heroic" efforts in the interest of those most in need of urgent care. And so his apparition would probably recoil at this reworking of his own inadequate first labors and at so much haste to take action destined only to be futile. It was because of bungled efforts like these that he had become the smirking naysayer, whose insistence on the uselessness of all quick travail had made him unbearable to his neurosurgical colleagues. Doctor Dominick was working hard to make the case for Haddington's point of view.

If Leroy were to survive long enough to have the CAT scan, and also make it to the operating room for surgery, then something needed to be done immediately to support his respirations, and also to counter the effects of brain swelling. Pressure was building up within the cranial cavity as his brain became waterlogged, "edematous," in reaction to the blood clot. The mounting intracranial pressure was interfering with his ability to breathe properly, and the clot, together with the swelling, was pushing the uncus against the midbrain. Instead of sliding Leroy into the CAT scanner where he would only suffocate, Doctor Dominick should have passed a plastic tube, an endotracheal tube, into his trachea.

Leroy could then be hooked up to a ventilating machine, a respirator, so that oxygen could be given, and by having the machine set to make him breathe rapidly, "hyperventilate," it would have also been possible to reduce the carbon dioxide levels in his lung and in his blood stream. Such a reduction of carbon dioxide can effectively lower intracranial pressure by reducing the state of distension of the cerebral arteries. Doctor Dominick was capable of performing an intubation, but did not understand how necessary it was. If he had ever heard, or read, that carbon dioxide, retained because of impaired respiration, causes the cerebral arteries to dilate and to take up more space, thereby adding to the mounting pressure, it did not spring to his mind right then. He certainly didn't act as one having the advantage of such knowledge. Also, he needed to give Leroy an intravenous injection of mannitol. That drug, a strong activator of urination, an "osmotic diuretic," by drawing water from the brain, would have further reduced the intracranial pressure for several hours. He had to have known about this treatment method. It's been commonplace for more than forty years. The problem, once again, was that he did not realize he was dealing with a condition calling for such treatment. The reasons for Leroy to die were mounting.

"Hey! Look what we've got!" was the way one very accommodating and discerning x-ray technician drew the attention of a neurosurgeon just happening to pass down his department corridor about fifteen minutes later.

The technician and Doctor Dominick had been studying the first CAT scan images to appear on the monitor screen and were marvelling at what they revealed of the size of an intracerebral blood clot, severe associated brain swelling, and a shift of brain tissue from right to left within Leroy's cranial cavity. Finally, there would be a much needed neurosurgical consultation, but it was not to be Doctor Dominick who hailed down this particular specialist on his way to review x-ray films of one of his own patients. It was the technician.

One brief glance at the monitor and the neurosurgeon

hurried into the room to yank Leroy from the machine, knowing full well, from only his quick study, that he would not be pleased with what he'd find. There lay a young black male, who after fifteen minutes in the scanner, without treatment or help to breathe, no longer responded except by generalized body stiffening. Both of his pupils were widely dilated and fixed to light. Only an occasional breath was still being drawn.

The neurosurgeon exploded. "What the hell is going on?"

"Glad you're here. I was going to call in a radiologist to have a look at the films," said Dominick.

"You've got to be kidding!"

And then he realized that Doctor Dominick surely wasn't.

There was no time to be further wasted locking on to Dominick with a disbelieving stare. Doctor Noble, the neurosurgeon, raced down the hall and returned in but a few moments with a laryngoscope and an endotracheal tube, the while having summoned an anaesthetist to come to the x-ray department. Leroy was intubated, attached to a ventilator, and rolled back to the emergency room where at the direction of Doctor Noble he was given an injection of cortisone. Cortisone doesn't do very much for brain swelling when it is secondary to head injury. Then why that particular drug? And still, why no mannitol, either? What was Doctor Noble thinking, or possibly, second thinking, as he rushed to and fro?

"I knew it all along. It's hopeless. I'm afraid there's nothing more we can do," opined Dominick.

"Right, Dominick. I'll leave a brief note."

Doctor Noble did as much, having undertaken only slight further examination of Leroy. Then, as suddenly as he had first appeared, he was gone.

What passed between those two doctors might satisfy very well the likes of Doctor Haddington, who if still hovering as some kind of a ghostly witness to all of this, would have initially been somewhat exasperated by as much dashing about between x-ray and the emergency room as had occurred, everybody seeming to be hell-bent upon trying to alter what he would consider an untreatable, irreversible, situation. The impatience of that old duffer for getting on with the declaration of Leroy's nonsalvageability notwithstanding, there still existed, albeit slim, another reality. Because of it, Doctor Noble, who unlike Doctor Dominick knew all the right moves and who might on noncritical review seem beyond reproach for his actions, must nevertheless share some of the responsibility for Leroy's death.

Doctor Noble's physical examination of Leroy had included an irrigation of his ear canals with ice water. In normal patients, certain eye movements occur in response to this maneuver, and these allow a doctor to determine whether or not the neuronal pathways of the brain stem are still intact. When such eye movements, called nystagmus, cannot be evoked by ice water irrigation, it is assumed that the brain stem has been damaged. Taken together with certain other findings, observations of this kind may even entitle an examiner to certify a patient as "brain dead." There are times when this means that further treatment may be withheld, and if the patient should then have a cardiac arrest, no effort will be made to resuscitate, provided that the family agrees to this course of action. Leroy's eyes had shown no response to the ice water irrigation.

While Doctor Noble performed his limited examination, Doctor Dominick took the nurses aside to comment on this unfortunate turn of events. From the beginning, he confided, or at least since Leroy had returned to the hospital, it had been obvious to him, things were not going to work out. The boy's fate had been sealed by the blow to his head. He had known it all along, but even if it were to be only for the sake of appearances, he had had to do everything that could possibly be done. He owed it to Leroy and to the family. Whatever the nurses thought, and it is not certain they did any thinking at all, they responded with nodding agreement. Events in the emergency room were proceeding in the Haddington tradition. The air was heavy with the mood and the expressions of hopelessness.

If one knows about matters of this kind, clearly it was not quite over. Instead of spending precious time to prove Leroy close to death, Doctor Noble might more usefully, and to his greater credit, have made further effort to save him. But before he tore off, he did nothing else.

Children, almost invariably, are extended the consideration of especially vigorous last measures of treatment in what may be their final moments. One would expect, at the very least, that Doctor Noble would have given Leroy some intravenous mannitol in an attempt to decompress his brain, by extracting some of its water content. That much was entirely feasible. Moreover, the dilatation of the pupils and the other signs of deterioration had only been present for a few minutes when he arrived on the scene. It is not very often that doctors have so early an opportunity to begin heroic salvage efforts. When such has been the case, they have been occasionally rewarded with surprisingly good results irrespective of abnormal ice water irrigation findings. One can find articles in the medical literature, especially about young patients, but even an occasional adult, who with fixed dilated pupils, treated promptly, have made a full recovery. One would also have expected him to give instructions regarding the need for Leroy to be hyperventilated in order to reduce his carbon dioxide levels, in a further effort to lower his intracranial pressure. Then, if any kind of favorable response did occur, such as a narrowing of his pupils, Leroy might be moved to the operating room for removal of the clot. There are even neurosurgeons who would remove the clot irrespective of how the patient might or might not react to such therapeutic trial measures, arguing that no purpose is served by wasting time awaiting encouraging indicators. After all, nothing could be lost by operating, and perhaps something could be gained.

What can be surmised from the unusual conduct of Doctor Noble following upon his almost reflex and efficiently conducted first efforts to resuscitate this patient? Certainly, he was not the neurosurgical counterpart of Doctor Dominick. To the contrary, he was neither incompetent nor lazy. Did he have second thoughts after sizing up the situation in which he, not formally invited to consult, had impetuously if well-meaningly inserted himself? Did he decide that his earlier intercession did not augur well for his self interest? After all, the chances were that Leroy could not be saved. So with that being the likely outcome why take the risk of further involvement? The less his good name was linked to this hospital record and to Doctor Dominick the better it might be for him. Doctor Dominick's management of the patient was patently so awful there was a significant chance of Dominick facing a lawsuit for losing a life which had been very easy to save. If Doctor Noble were to implicate himself any further either by medical treatment or by operating upon Leroy, the possibility of his being tied to the earlier tainted care would be increased. He probably didn't want such a linkage. He could hardly afford to share, any more than necessary, in guilt by association with Dominick. He may very well have also wanted that his ministrations appear on the record as having been rendered during a time frame characterized by his own descriptive entries as terminal. So he deprived Leroy of medication with mannitol, of hyperventilation, of emergency operation, of a chance, albeit meager, to survive. He abandoned him, managing finally to contribute only a forlorn and questionably accurate, hopeless prognosis. In the end, however much Leroy was still in need of better care and an operation, what it probably came down to was Doctor Noble's own needs. Apparently, they counted for more. It was necessary, most of all, to distance himself from Dominick. It looks like Doctor Noble ran for cover.

Later on, the family gathered in the intensive care unit—mother, sister, grandparents, and some young friends. Doctor Dominick appeared and held forth that in that part of the hospital Leroy would receive every possible attention in the hope of his recovery, but the outlook was grim indeed. There was little chance he could pull through. Bleeding, unluckily, had now started up so deeply within his brain that no neurosurgeon could reach it without causing unacceptable damage, a degree of damage incompatible with normal function. The new bleeding was approaching that stage in which matters would soon be irreversible. All of this, to confirm what had been his initial worst suspicions, had been demonstrated by the CAT scan, and was substantiated by the extreme size of the hemorrhage. It is unsettling to wonder how many times Doctor Dominick had spouted similar nonsense, had played out this same role.

What the CAT scan actually showed was a clot just beneath the surface of the brain, on the non dominant or less important right side, and in the temporal lobe, a place where speech, intellectual function, movement, sensation, and probably vision would not have been affected by either the clot or any surgical effort to remove it. It was, in fact, so close to the surface, that as the coroner observed later, it would have found its own way out, if only an exit had been provided. Nor was Leroy being damaged by progressive bleeding. The clot, as is usual in this circumstance, was self contained. Bleeding had stopped almost as soon as it had begun. The brain, however, had reacted over time to the hemorrhage with progressive swelling. It was this edema which was the threat to life. Although the edema, by causing a build-up of pressure, had even stopped the bleeding, it had also interfered with blood flow to the brain, to produce various symptoms of that "ischemia" as well as the problem of uncal herniation. Doctor Haddington's peculiar ideas notwithstanding, this condition of Leroy had from its outset constituted the circumstance most commonly regarded by neurosurgeons as an emergency requiring immediate operation, an operation often yielding a favorable outcome.

The next day, a nurse recorded in the hospital chart that Leroy's mother, advised of the hopelessness of his condition, had given Doctor Dominick permission for his organs to be donated as part of the hospital transplant program. The transplant team was notified and explanations of what was to follow were passed on to the family. This should not be. Among the many other things that Doctor Dominick did not seem to know, or knew and tried to circumvent, was a requirement that in cases of possible death by manslaughter the body must be examined by the coroner, and therefore its organs are not available for donation. Leroy had been the victim of what stood to be a case of fatal assault. Protection of the rights of the person to be charged with that crime required a full examination of all body parts of the deceased to determine if death was truly by assault, or some other cause. The medical director of the hospital got wind of this irregularity just in time to stop the transplant team from proceeding.

Such haste to seek after Leroy's organs needs looking at. Organs are "harvested" only after all of the final criteria for brain death are met. Then, with permission of the family, life supports can be withdrawn. But Leroy only needed respiratory assistance. He could breathe a little on his own. His electroencephalogram showed that he still had some brain wave activity. It was not necessary to use medication to support his blood pressure. The criteria for brain death were simply not there. Even when they are, a physician usually gives the family a little breathing room before such discussions are held. Fatal injuries are totally unanticipated when they strike. They are shocking enough without having some strange doctor rush at the family precipitously in what may seem like a hasty move to forage for spare body parts. Although preliminary discussions are commonly entered into before the full deterioration of brain death has occurred, usually they are not hurried along in a case like this. It was all too soon. People have to have more time to adjust, especially to the impending loss of a child. They have barely endurable levels of grief and require consideration. Nor is any prospective recipient of an organ brought legitimately closer to having his or her needs met by some doctor jumping the gun with premature and, under these circumstances, oddly presented illegal urgings for such a bequest.

What might Doctor Dominick really have been up to? Did he think that by parcelling Leroy's organs off in so many different directions, the role he himself had played in bringing on his death could be obscured? Was his ploy no more than an enterprise to prevent the coroner from discovering what had been a missed opportunity for surgical removal of the clot? Was Leroy intended by him to simply disappear among the legions of those prematurely dead and harvested for transplantation? As it turned out, the family first began to wonder about Dominick on learning from the medical director of his impropriety in approaching them this way. They became further suspicious on appreciating the obvious contrast between the willingness of Doctor Dominick to talk to them now at great length versus his earlier elusiveness, if not complete absence, during those critical moments when Leroy needed his attention and they in turn might have benefitted from a better description of his medical condition. If Doctor Dominick had it in mind that this was his moment, after the fact, to make a favorable impression by projecting the image of a concerned, knowledgeable, physician, he was dead wrong. By being so different from what he had been before he had become transparent, even to simple folk like the members of Leroy's family.

When everything is going well, such an incompetent doctor, working as an emergency care provider, can get by on a little know-how and a certain kind of personality. The institutionally decked out, dead earnest or upbeat doctors of the E.R. may carry on in spite of their professional limitations. And when things do not turn out well, it is only on rare occasions that there is detection of the inadequacies of such doctors. Even something as grossly wrong as the treatment of Leroy will not usually draw any official attention.

There are other doctors like Dominick. Some of them enter medical school not because they want to practice medicine and to care for people. They go to medical school because they want to be doctors. There are obvious advantages to being a doctor. We know them all. What such physicians do manage to learn in school is retained only as long as it need be, for satisfactory spewing back during examinations. After medical school, if they should go on to graduate study in some specialty, again they learn only so much and for so long as may be necessary to pass certain additional examinations. Then, their attitude is that they can afford to forget, and they bother themselves little to learn anything more, unless periodically required to submit to re-evaluations. What they do, primarily, is enjoy those advantages associated with being a doctor. Even if, as it can easily turn out, they wind up not having much taste for the labors and the life style of medical practice, they stick with it, anyway. It is simply too late in life for anything else. Besides which, by then they have invested too many years and considerable money, having not uncommonly assumed major debt to become doctors. Making money can be their end-all as well as their beginning. Such physicians, in particular, need watching over. It is possible, as well, that no one ever took pains to advise them, when starting out, of the arduous aspects of medical practice and of the need to maintain high levels of proficiency. They may come, therefore, when hard pressed by these built in rigors, to finally resent being a doctor as they are subjected to such stresses. There are doctors who seem to direct that resentment toward everyone around them, including their patients.

No purpose is served by searching for the origins, the circumstances, or the social underpinnings, of the motivation to choose medicine as a career. Why should one? Is it possible to change any of that? Hardly. And every one of us can either start out with behavioral or character flaws or acquire them along the way. Everybody also winds up differently, uniquely. There lies the problem in present day clinical medicine. It operates by the unpredictable whim, the brilliance, or the frailty of human beings. And so there can be nothing consistent about it.

5

Charles

STANDARD

*Patients having intracerebral clots associated with midline shifts
of five millimeters or more should be operated upon promptly for
clot removal. In the event of unilateral pupillary enlargement,
surgery should be performed as an emergency in conjunction
with acceptable measures for reducing the intracranial pressure.*

It wasn't the same policeman. It wasn't even the same part
of town. But for Charles Kassim, it all fit together. It might
just do that, for someone like him, staggering and confused. The union medical clinic would later attest to his problems with alcohol. They were the likely reason he had not shown
up for work, and by that afternoon had already been arrested
and released from jail. Charles had assaulted one of his neighbors and had attempted to force his entry into a nearby store
just closed for the day. Now, in quite a different place, remote
from where he lived, he was headed for trouble again, thinking
this was the very same nasty cop who had jailed him four
hours earlier. Officer Young, however, was not that other Philadelphia policeman; and he did not take kindly to being called
a "mother fucker," or to being held responsible for events of
that day about which he had absolutely no knowledge. He was
also not prepared to make special allowance for the unstable
mental condition of the dark figure screaming something unin-
telligible about justice and having his revenge. So with just a
single carefully aimed swing of his nightstick, he had Charles
down in the gutter. He did it non-lethally by a strike to his legs.
Charles, seeking to avenge his earlier detention, had picked on

the wrong policeman, and not only because this one had never encountered him before, but because he was very sturdy, very unforgiving, and very capable of changing the direction of troublemakers much more substantially constructed than this little man from Sierra Leone.

Charles' apprehension, though forcible, was conducted in public, and so it had to go strictly by the book. On the other hand, no one can ever know precisely what happened to him later on, when he was confined to his solitary jail cell. In that place there were no disinterested witnesses.

Before this second incarceration, two arresting officers took Charles to a local hospital for examination. It was observed that he had bruises of the lower limbs where struck by the officer's nightstick. Except for his reliance upon certain offensively couched declarations, delivered in English, he used a language no one could comprehend, but it was decided, nonetheless, that he was unable to make those kinds of response appropriate to his circumstance. The diagnosis was of a mental disorder secondary to alcohol. Then, having received sedation, he was taken off to prison once more.

The next morning he was found in his cell unconscious, trousers soiled, capable of making only right sided limb movements. Returned to the same hospital for re-evaluation, a paralysis of his left side was confirmed. Also, he was showing no responses except to painful stimulation. Blood pressure, pulse, and respiration, the so called "vital signs," were normal. He had soiled his trousers with both urine and feces, commonly taken indications of there having been an epileptic seizure.

Should the emergency room physician be faulted for writing in the record "no signs of trauma"? That person was only a part- time, moonlighting dermatologist, trained to be an obstetrician. After all, within an hour, a highly qualified neurosurgeon would render an opinion which was no different. Both of them would fail to take the brief amount of time required to do no more than see his bruises or especially to palpate the top of Charles' head for tell-tale signs of bogginess, the soft tissue evidence of bleeding into the scalp, secondary to a head injury. To what avail all of their laborious studying over so many post-graduate years, when these two physicians were utterly blind to the simple fact that Charles, for persisting in his contrary ways, had now the signs of having been beaten about the head at the hands of the police, in retaliation for continuing to abuse and to taunt them, even from out his jail cell?

In any event, as is often the case, the failure to perform a proper physical examination might possibly have been remedied by special testing, including a CAT scan of his head. What was done for Leroy, but much too late, was done promptly for Charles and presumably, should have benefitted him. There is, of course, that assumption in clinical medicine of a benefit to be anticipated by the testing of patients. Actually, the sick are often described as having had the benefit of this or that test or procedure. Hardly can it be said, however, that Charles was in fact so privileged, when it becomes known that for all of this kind of sophisticated testing the evidence of his having sustained a head injury was once more overlooked. The doctors who failed to observe the obvious external indications of a head injury were not to have their inexcusable error made up for by their detection, in the CAT scan, of those same important signs. Although there were multiple areas of scalp hemorrhage to be seen in the scan, as well as two linear skull fractures, the only abnormality noted by the neurosurgeon and the emergency room doctor was a clot within the right side of Charles' brain. And the hospital radiologist, who later reviewed the same study, came to no different conclusion. Our newer technology, it would seem, does not yet reliably compensate for the failure of physicians to make appropriate physical examinations, or to draw important clinical distinctions, as long as the capacity to interpret what is produced by machines is also a flawed human endeavor. Computerized radiological imaging or CAT scanning is a critically essential method for reaching a diagnosis but is lacking in interpretive automation. This is particularly unfortunate because, increasingly, reliance upon that same technology has inspired a laxity, if not actual rejection, of traditional clinical examining skills. We have been abandoned more and more to devices still not capable of automatically serving up specific, necessary, often urgently needed diagnoses and yet because of the very presence of such machines, physicians no longer bother to examine patients as carefully as they used to. In fact, recent studies have shown that the majority of both doctors in training and graduate specialists in internal medicine do not even know how to use a stethoscope properly.

This neurosurgeon, a Doctor Gamble, failing to detect either clinical or radiographic signs of head injury, the actual cause of the hemorrhage, opined that Charles had bled spontaneously into the right side of his brain from an abnormal blood vessel. He suspected bleeding from an "aneurysm." Patients do bleed from so-called aneurysms because in such instances, structurally defective arterial walls near the sites at which arteries commonly branch, may balloon out to become small or large parchment thin blebs which finally burst under the pressure of the blood within them. Aneurysms generally require surgical clipping to eliminate the risk of further bleeding because a second hemorrhage carries a high risk of death. Surgery may also be necessary if blood clots accumulate in the brain and have to be removed, in order to prevent fatal brain swelling and herniation secondary to increased intracranial pressure. In that event, the clinical considerations regarding management of a blood clot within the brain are not much different than they were for Leroy. The clot in Charles' brain, as in the case of Leroy, was large enough to produce symptoms. It was causing marked pressure, to the extent that a fluid-containing space, the third ventricle, one of the brain chambers in which the cerebrospinal fluid is formed, was shifted away from its usual position in the middle of the brain. Under pressure, both from the clot and the brain swelling associated with it, the third ventricle was displaced far to the left of the midline of the cranial cavity. These abnormalities were evident in the CAT scan. It was extremely unusual, in fact, by virtue of their severity, that these disturbances had not already caused uncal herniation and irreversible damage to the brain stem. Fanciful, perhaps, to so regard Charles in his dire situation, but on this small point one might consider him to have been quite lucky.

Doctor Gamble summoned a radiologist to the hospital and took Charles back to x-ray to search for the suspected aneurysm by performing an arteriogram. An arteriogram is an x-ray study involving the injection of a radio-opaque substance into the blood stream. Such material contains iodine and blocks the passage of x-rays permitting a detailed depiction of arteries as well as other blood vessels of the brain. But nothing was seen except for the displacement of blood vessels away from the clot. There was no aneurysm or any other kind of blood vessel abnormality. The radiologist who performed the procedure observed that certain arteries, ordinarily located in the middle of the brain, the anterior cerebral arteries, were shifted towards the left, consistent with the displacement of the third ventricle, as had been previously detected in the CAT scan. Thus, neither the neurosurgeon nor the radiologist could come up with a reason for Charles to have had a hemorrhage. And they did not re-examine the patient or his earlier performed CAT scan in an effort to seek out those clues that were discernible had they but heeded the physical and prior CAT scan evidences of a beating. Charles, who was no more responsive, was given an injection of cortisone. The neurosurgeon and the radiologist took off for home.

When Mrs. Kassim arrived at the hospital, her husband was under police guard. One of life's oddities that a man carried off to the hospital paralyzed and stuporous from a hemorrhage in his brain should need round the clock police surveillance! It had not been easy for her during the first two days of her husband's disappearance. She had gotten no information as to why he was missing. Summoned finally to the police station, she found that the lieutenant there could say no more than would the officer at her husband's bedside about what had happened to Charles. Other than his having been arrested for overtly hostile behavior, both policemen were tight-lipped. The nurses and the resident doctors did mention something about his possibly having had an epileptic type seizure in jail, brought on, in all likelihood, by a brain hemorrhage. When she offered information that he had been under treatment for high blood pressure, someone suggested that the hypertension might very well have been the reason for him to bleed. Nothing more was confided to her about his condition. It seems that no one bothered to even puzzle any further about the reason for his having had a brain hemorrhage. There was nothing for her to do but what devoted wives have always done under such circumstances. She held his hand, and sat beside his bed wondering what was to befall them next.

As she stared at his face, it was clear to her that he looked a little different about the eyes. The white of the right one, the sclera, showed a reddish discoloration. Blood from the underlying fracture of his orbital bone had been slowly seeping across it. Sad that an uneducated woman from Sierra Leone should be that much better at clinical observation than all of those highly trained doctors. Continuing to fix upon him, and still wondering about the meaning of the bloody eye, she began after a while to doze, until awakened by his voice. He wanted a "Pepsi." He was back in Sierra Leone, and he wanted a "Pepsi." Then, he was no longer in Sierra Leone. He was very much there again, in Philadelphia, and insisted upon knowing why those policemen had come into his jail cell, and would not leave off from beating him. He asked for his children, then, over and over, he wanted to know why the cops had beaten him so. His wife did not summon a nurse. She got him his Pepsi from a vending machine downstairs and then watched as he grasped it with the right hand, his remaining good one, and proceeded without hesitation or difficulty to gulp the soda down. "Why," she questioned the police guard, "would anyone beat up my husband at the jail?" "Oh, he's out of his head!" was her answer. But Charles kept at it, and now under the stimulating effect of one well caffeinated Pepsi Cola, continued to demand his own explanation, sometimes in English, and also in their own language.

"Out of his head"? Not really so assuredly for this police officer that he did not hasten to telephone his superior that one Charles Kassim was now very much awake and screaming like all bloody murder, his Léonese charges of police brutality. He need not have been so concerned. Charles, receiving no real treatment for his swollen brain, and soon no longer stimulated by the Pepsi Cola he had fortuitously self-prescribed, became drowsy and slept once more.

When the nurses, over the next two days would pinch him, he would rouse to take fluids by mouth, and according to his family talk about things back home as if he were there, but he did not speak further about being in jail, or of what had happened to him at the hands of the police. Only a doctor who could examine a patient properly, or look at a CAT scan and recognize the signs of injury, would be able to know that. There were no such doctors taking care of Charles. Nevertheless, he had managed to have his say, and however brief it was, it would be sufficient to raise a certain kind of concern, but not one that was medical.

"What are his chances?" That question, according to a police report, was put to Doctor Gamble by two investigating police lieutenants the next day. There is no record of anything being offered to this doctor by the police as an account of how Charles had spent his time in jail. Nor is there any written indication of questions asked of the police by Doctor Gamble, concerning this obscure period of detention. The official summary of this police interview reflects only that the doctor held out little hope for his patient's recovery. There is no reference, either, by way of any entry in any document, of Charles' laying claim to a beating, or of his wife's recounting of it. Would it not seem reasonable to expect that if there were the least concern for this man's well being, at least some questioning would have been entered into by someone regarding the mysterious cause of the condition about which chances for recovery were being asked, estimated, and minimized? Unless that particular subject was strictly taboo, the more usual line of inquiry would start with "What's he got? What's wrong with him?" rather than "Will he make it?." Or, was the subject of a beating at the hands of the police not in fact prohibited, only the writing down of any mention of it? Considering the fact that Mrs. Kassim, to some degree, had already gone public with at least a question of police brutality, how could any discussion between the police and her husband's doctor not include at least passing reference to the claim of his having received a head injury? Of course, if Charles were to die, he being the only person entitled to make that accusation, however credibly, it would be difficult for the same charge to be levelled by anyone else. Especially out of his wife's mouth, it would be second hand and suspect. Like as not, the police came away from their meeting with the doctor their purpose served and their concerns allayed. They stood to be reassured by the doctor's prediction that Charles was going to die. With so many people apt to say that Charles was either acting crazy, or was stuporous during his final days, it is hardly possible anyone would seriously consider he had even made any kind of valid dying declaration of the assault upon him. What the police would want to happen is more than suspect. The question which lingers concerns the possibility that a doctor, harboring some kind of secret sympathy or prejudice, might be moved enough by that influence to ignore his professional obligations to a patient. That question needs looking at in the light of certain peculiar actions and statements of the neurosurgeon.

There was no aneurysm. No abnormality of that kind had been detected in the arteriogram. Accordingly, there was no need to perform an operation for the prevention of further bleeding. If an aneurysm had been found, the neurosurgeon would necessarily have considered surgery to remove the blood clot and to place a metal clip on the neck of the aneurysm to exclude it from the circulation so that it would not bleed again. But what about the blood clot? Was there any less reason to remove it, simply because, to the mind of the neurosurgeon, it was not possible to know how it had come to exist in Charles' brain? However it had come to be there, its effects would be the same. It was producing pressure, swelling, impairment of blood flow, a lowering of vital tissue tensions of oxygen, and even harmful acidic conditions of brain tissue.

Neurosurgeons always remove such large, pressure producing, symptomatic blood clots once they cause major shifts of midline brain structures and if they seriously threaten to cause coma, or that much feared condition of uncal herniation. Also, in advance of surgery, such doctors administer the drug mannitol to reduce the intracranial pressure. For Charles Kassim no such medication was ordered, and no operation was being planned. What could be the reason? Should it be considered that between the time the neurosurgeon saw the results of the arteriogram, and the time he decided there was nothing to be offered this patient, he had heard, possibly from some detective, of the wife's charge that her husband had been assaulted by the police?

How reliable may a comfortably well-off doctor be in the care of a poor, African, lawbreaking drunkard, if he does not customarily take care of such people and if personal safety or law and order have become his obsession? Given the opportunity of influencing some future conflict between those who protect and secure his privileged order and some irascible foreign troublemaker, might he take that occasion to act to the detriment of such a person, even if that troublemaker happens to be his patient?

Years later, Doctor Gamble would say that Charles was either a "vegetable" or not possible of being made quite normal again, when he had given up on the prospects of treating him any further. A "vegetable." Can any human being, at any level of existence, be called a vegetable? Most of us have a good idea of what is implied by that pronouncement. It is something even less than life in the vegetative state which is a life unknowing and without deliberate purpose, a life of respiration, blood flow, and bodily eliminations. The intended implication falls short of the mark if we summon up the image of any vegetable. After all, what form of life in the plant world is capable of even those residual, yet still complex life support functions? And what is really known of the kinds of dreams such humans who "vegetate" are capable of in their varied states of unconsciousness? Does the average head of lettuce have them? Or can anyone honestly say they are truly an insignificant experience for the dreamer? And do not such patients who have "vegetated" awaken occasionally from those lower levels of being, only to ridicule the arrogant conceit of the medical doomsayers who predicted their demise, by revealing they have spent years, not only at dreaming, but at taking in much of what was happening around them. They stood a watchful vigil in their so-called comas. It's taken us some time but we've learned to label their impudent recoveries as "awakenings," emergences from what is called a coma vigil.

Hardly, in all fairness, could it be honestly said that during the first five days of his hospitalization Charles was in that poor a condition. Actually, he was taking food by mouth and quite aggressively so. It was a diet his doctor had even written orders for in the hospital chart! He was right handed, but paralyzed only in his left limbs. The right upper and lower extremities moved normally. Those retained capabilities were indications that his brain stem, as well as his left cerebrum, the important side of his brain, were reasonably intact. This was known, also, because he spoke quite well, even though it was in his native tongue and he gave evidence of being confused. The speech centers were therefore intact and complex ideational thought processes were both feasible and demonstrable. He swore oaths in Léonese. Occasionally, he yanked the catheter out of his bladder, and had to be restrained so as to keep him in bed. Some vegetable!

And if the neurosurgeon did not believe it possible to return him to his "normal" prior state of being, who has ever suggested that medical treatment be restricted to that objective? Quite commonly, reality forces both doctors and patients to settle for a lot less.

Then there looms the larger question. To whom, conceivably, would belong the right of letting him die by neglect? Is the doctor, alone, or even the wife, or anyone at all ever individually privileged to make that kind of decision? Could it possibly be appropriate for a doctor to suggest such an option be acted upon, much less even entertained, when variable degrees of improvement under correct treatment could be reasonably anticipated, and the patient was being observed to still retain a wide range of functional activity? Medical actions and considerations were afoot that betrayed the presence of motivations quite distinct from those of caring for this patient. And they relied for their sway upon the ignorance and the disadvantaged positions of the Kassims.

Charles would certainly not improve without treatment. Slowly, as time passed, he became less responsive. When he began to bring up his food and to refuse his oral feedings, he was started on intravenous fluids. Gradually, day by day, he showed fewer spontaneous movements. By the fourth day following his admission to the hospital, he moved only when stimulated painfully over the right side of the body. He made no further effort to speak. He had been silenced. This was not patient care. It was a malignant charade.

Time slipped by, and the written record of his hospitalization, the medical chart, was memorializing it as the final episode of a life terminating in a condition said to be medically and surgically untreatable. Diligently, the neurosurgeon recorded his daily insistence of the hopelessness of it all. To that end, on the third day, he supported those pessimistic predictions with objective evidence. He had had the CAT scan repeated. The shifting of midline brain structures was increased. The edema had become much more extensive and yet the clot was not any larger in its dimensions. It was of the same size, and by its superficial presentation, it fairly begged of removal. Clearly, it was the clot which was making things worse primarily by causing an increase in the swelling of the brain around it. Most neurosurgeons would have considered those images a demand for operation and it would be an irresistible one. So too, probably, would Doctor Gamble, but in some other setting. Here, it would seem, he was constrained from doing what was indicated by the override of another calling. This doctor, trained for long years to believe he could make a difference when others less knowledgeable might think there was nothing to be done, was now at work only to build a record of despair. His was a different agenda. He merely left a note that there was CAT scan evidence of further deterioration.

In the early hours of the morning of the sixth day Doctor Gamble was awakened by a nurse reporting a sudden change in the patient's condition. The right pupil was slightly larger than the left, and was reacting only sluggishly to light. Uncal herniation had started. The nurse was instructed to administer lasix by subcutaneous injection. This drug, a diuretic agent, is used to increase the output of urine. It is capable of reducing intracranial pressure, but its action is mild, slowly reached, and somewhat uncertain. It is definitely not the drug of choice for brain swelling in an urgent clinical situation. Mannitol, once more, was the drug to have been ordered. It is administered intravenously and is just about routinely prescribed when a neurosurgical patient begins to herniate. It seems that there was an apparent need on this particular morning at three AM, to show that at least something was being done to prevent Charles from dying on the spot. But the much less suitable medication was given, along with oxygen by nasal cannula. The nurse was also instructed not to awaken Doctor Gamble again, should the patient's condition deteriorate further. And she was reminded that if that slippage did occur, there was to be no "code," that is no urgent signalling of other physicians or personnel to re-suscitate the patient. Charles was to pass without further medical intercession.

Real doctors order that mannitol be infused while they rush to the hospital for patients such as this who are beginning to herniate. They summon anesthesiologists so that oxygen may be given by endotracheal tube, after an emergency intubation is performed, and then hyperventilation is also carried out to reduce the intracranial pressure. They don't just give token oxygen through the nose. They do not stay at home in bed, perhaps guiltily avoiding the stare of a patient's dilating pupil. Neurosurgeons have come to understand that pupillary dilatation is an alarm signal. It must be responded to quickly and properly. And they will probably have to operate in a circumstance like this in order to remove the blood clot. Doctor Gamble had reason to hide from eyes that could seem to sense a purpose for his ignoring their signal of distress.

When he arrived at the hospital the next day, what Doctor Gamble saw was unexpected. Rather than fixed dilated pupils and other signs of further worsening, he was confronted with evidence of improvement. Charles was not alert, or less paralyzed, or even responding better to painful stimuli, but the previously enlarged pupil was at least back down to normal size and once more it was reactive. So this neurosurgeon was put on notice very clearly, unmistakably, that Charles' condition was still reversible. And in fact, since it had been feasible to induce improvement by injecting so weak a diuretic agent as lasix, rather than mannitol, the stronger drug generally required to produce an effect, it was demonstrated that Charles was eminently treatable. He had passed what is known as a therapeutic test. Clinical assessment of this kind is routinely performed by neurosurgeons as part of the need to distinguish those patients who can be saved from those who cannot. If after the administration of a drug, or the institution of respiratory assistance, patients show favorable pupillary change, or other evidences of improved responsivity, doctors generally consider that further treatment, possibly to include surgery, is warranted, whereas failure to improve may be taken as a sign of irreversible brain damage, and except where children are concerned, operation is generally regarded as futile.

Doctor Gamble did not read the signs that way. He was not about to take Charles to any operating room. Under prodding, however, from a somewhat knowledgeable resident physician, he ordered that Charles be intubated for ventilatory support. If the medical record were to be read by someone who knew nothing about neurosurgery, it would appear that things were being done for Charles. That dissemblance might come in handy down the road should anyone raise questions. Nevertheless, a little oxygen, a machine for supporting respiration, and a mild medication to increase the urinary output, whatever their usefulness might be over the short term in prolonging life or prettying up the record, they were no real substitute for mannitol and removal of the blood clot causing the brain to swell and to herniate.

Also, as if to suggest his hand in all of this was incidental or adjunct, Doctor Gamble entered into the progress record his concurrence with the treatment being rendered by the residents and other doctors. He had made himself an outsider, offering commentary upon a downward clinical spiral, inevitable by its nature, but still being heroically delayed through the admirable intercessions of a dedicated medical team. The hospital chart would become a tribute to the dogged, devoted, determination on the part of interns and residents to sustain life, and an example of how doctors never give up, even when it might seem wasteful of effort and prospectively nonproductive for them to carry on. Charles was launched, essentially, on a no-fault trajectory into the next world, and he was to be considered fortunate to have been so well attended on that last journey.

The result was predictable. When finally his pupils became widely dilated, it was only minutes beyond that terminal expression of astonishment to a full cardiac arrest. The ventilator was turned off. Charles breathed no more, and then perhaps, certain others could breathe all the more easily.

His life. Valued so differently. A nuisance to his neighbors. Unreliable at work. A boozer. Unpredictable as a clinic patient. His wife's cross, but beloved by her nonetheless. He was known for years by so many people who were entitled to be resentful of him, and yet not one of them had ever wished him dead. Even the policemen responsible for the assault upon him had not intended that he die. Only a person knowing him the most briefly, but entrusted with the responsibility for saving his life, was to act as though he placed no value upon it. And for such a one, what concerns of his needed such strong address that they overwhelmed his medical obligations?

Could Doctor Gamble's hand in this ever be truly known? Physicians would be the only ones able to understand the woeful inadequacy of the treatment rendered by him. But he could be confident that if the matter were to somehow attract attention, other surgeons would only view it, at worst, in terms of clinical oversight or an unfortunate but acceptable lapse of judgment. And most medical doctors who did have any familiarity with Charles' hospitalization would not even know the principles of neurosurgery well enough to suspect that an almost certain major recovery had been deliberately thwarted. So there was nothing for him to worry about on that score. But how about feelings of guilt? An unease to last, perhaps, the rest of his life? That sense of failed moral or personal responsibility, said by some to be a human attribute, yet argued by others to require urging or inculcation? The notable thing about guilt is the ofttimes ease with which the sense of it is carried or shirked. And so when Doctor Gamble was held to at least a legal accounting by being sued he hardly fretted over it.

What was achieved by this deadly neglect? Is it to be understood only by some bizarre, irresistible, or mean kind of satisfaction derived from it? Is it just to be explained by the uniquely peculiar, innate, and disturbed psyche of the perpetrator? But, why seek other than certain, unfortunately commonplace reasons?

It happened so that Doctor Gamble could discharge an animosity. And if at the same time, by his deliberate act of omission, he could fancy himself in league with whatever it was he counted on, or catered to, and which to his thinking was at risk, then so much more his calamitous inclination.

Who was this Doctor Gamble? He was another. He was Gambozelian. As some Boland or Gumble may spend lifetimes hiding from their Landsky and Goldman selves, for Gambozelian too, life was but a masquerade. But to be Gamble means having to be more and to do more than would one for whom that identity came by easy inheritance. Gambozelian had had to work hard for passage as Gamble. It was an uphill struggle of both self-avoidance and denial to seem the casual, respected, privileged Doctor Gamble. Name change and appropriate accoutrements had been easily enough arranged for. Money and an advantageous marriage also came readily to an aggressive, smart, newly made neurosurgeon. But every day, to be someone one is really not, is a different matter. And finally, there may come the time when such a "newly made" person may be stirred to hate the self, the true self, the one always somehow insinuating its reminder that there can never really be a Gamble. Such self disgust can be easily deflected, turned away, and directed instead at anything standing to jeopardize or to so much as ruffle the world of the false Gamble. A true Gamble, of course, doesn't have to concern himself with such considerations. He takes his station for granted and makes his way by means of what may be an ill deserved but nonetheless natural, effortless, and confident self-satisfaction. A Gambozelian, on the other hand, has to implement the dogged stubbornness of an ambitious Armenian to be not only Gamble, but to see to it that no one unsettles the special society in which he conceals himself. Whereas bona fide Gambles are inclined to be casual about their status and the disposition of most things, Gambozelian Gambles are extreme advocates of the law and order which secures them. Having deserted their own kind, they care not for them either. They are embarrassed by such people, may even despise them. Hardly then could it be expected there would be any regard at all for the rights of someone so unstable, so threatening, and so very different, as a Charles Kassim.

There are nonhuman life forms which exist nowadays only by the deference or pleasure of our species, the one said to be most endowed with intelligence. It is becoming its prerogative to will the destiny of many things understood by it. So much for what was once competitive in nature. What lives, what dies, can be a matter of some impersonal, calculating, human decision to act or to leave well enough alone. This corner of the universe has moved, as foreseen by H.G. Wells, considerably beyond most forms of natural control. We have meddled with it.

The human species has also inclined to see itself by certain less than subtle distinctions from other creatures, and to be unsettled by any seeming similarity. It does not admire, and is often hostile to, those aspects of human behavior which remind us of much simpler codes of natural conduct governing the ways of other life forms, which were also ours until we became "civilized." That is, up to when the emotional or aggressive side of sublimated man became goal oriented, or structured to an acceptable level in all kinds of ritualized activities.

But the old ways can never be fully exorcised. There are parts of the brain, the older parts, that are home eternal to them. They are controlled now by higher brain centers of younger vintage, but still, often to the general chagrin, that raging, revelling, spontaneous side of the human character does manage to erupt unpredictably. There are also occasions when its suppression by the higher centers is suspended during intoxication, or sexual activity, or herdlike participation in sports or military endeavors, and it manages to reveal itself. Arthur Koestler called this side of human nature "a ghost in the machine." Overtly displayed, quite depending upon the circumstance, it may be lauded, taken in good humor, resented, or condemned. Our attitudes regarding it are conditioned by variable social guidelines. Living is now quite carefully orchestrated.

Charles Kassim was that old, deeply rooted, unpredictable, and primitive side of man. Doctor Gamble, his ultimate censor, may have seemed impassive, yet he was an agent for the higher cerebral expression of a sophisticated, selective, and carefully directed violence. His newer type of aggression, in spite of its overwhelming power, is apt to be condoned or to go without notice by tacit social convention and understanding. Not surprisingly, the wild side of man, like the wild side of nature about him, is really no match for the evolved cunning or inscrutability of people like Doctor Gamble.

What should be regretted more, the passing of a Charles Kassim or the prevailing of a Doctor Gamble? When the roguish, rough hewn debauchery of an incorrigible Charles Kassim is confronted, does it really disturb us more than the self-serving, unruffled, vindictiveness of a Doctor Gamble? Which is worse, what once we were, or what too many of us have managed to become?

6

José

STANDARD

A neurosurgical consultant should make every reasonable effort to obtain a reliable account of the symptoms of head injured patients. The neurosurgeon must re-examine and re-evaluate head injured patients who have altered levels of consciousness on at least a daily basis or more frequently if necessary and personally review their x-rays and imaging studies. Patients having the signs or symptoms of increased intracranial pressure must be treated for it with known to be effective measures.

There was no neurosurgeon willing to testify on his behalf with the exception of the one man whose name also appeared in the hospital chart. Doctor Samuelson's treatment of José Pollenco was that bad. It is customary for any number of neurosurgeons to defend a colleague even when the care he has rendered is quite obviously inconsistent with how neurosurgeons ordinarily practice, but in this instance the only support Doctor Samuelson could muster was that of kind words from Doctor Taylor, a close friend and also a neurosurgeon. Taylor, following his own schedule, had turned up finally at the hospital hours after the last and final call for help from Doctor Samuelson had been put out, unavailingly, by an alarmed resident doctor and the nurses. He arrived only in time to witness the boy's final moments. Doctor Taylor, for lack of any particular expertise to qualify him as especially knowing in this matter, was presented to the conservative, blue collar jury more as a war hero than as a learned neurosurgeon. During World War II he had been a stateside air corps radio operator. It was legitimate, therefore, to the mind of Doctor Samuelson's lawyer, that

Doctor Taylor be known to the court as an aviator much deco-
rated for his exploits over Germany at the tail gun of a B-17.
Praise the lord! Pass the ammunition! And let Doctor Samuelson
off the hook in spite of what he had failed to do in regard to
José Pollenco.

Doctor Samuelson, also straining through a mighty effort
not to seem immodest, confessed to his own warrior role as a
military officer. That glory was won, in point of fact, as a re-
serve officer in the coast guard after the cessation of hostilities,
during which time he attended medical school at government
expense. The legal strategy was to envelop him and his defend-
ing cohort in the flag, to attack the plaintiff's expert by any and
all means, and to stymie any comprehensive presentation or
explanation of the hospital record from being made to the jury.
Nothing else could work. Certainly not any alibi which Doctor
Samuelson might offer up for what had happened to his patient
during the time he could not be reached by anyone at the hospital.

José, fifteen years old, had returned to his mother's home
at three o'clock of a July morning, clothing torn and body covered with bruises and abrasions. He had never gotten as far as
his girl friend's house for which he had set out at 8 o'clock of
the previous evening. His mother found him crawling about on
the living room floor in search of a shoe no one ever found.
That activity was not particularly well organized and was interrupted by vomiting, complaints of headache, and a strongly
expressed resentment for some person by the name of Rosa,
whom he accused of ejecting him from a car moving rather
rapidly down an unidentified Detroit back alley.

It would be nice if certain kids didn't really ever have to
be kids at all. Their growing pains are usually worse for parent
than child. Exasperated once more by this boy's foolishness,
but nonetheless caring and concerned for her son, Mrs. Pollenco
managed to get him to the emergency room with the assistance
of a neighbor. A CAT scan was done and interpreted as normal,
but nevertheless José was admitted to the hospital by the emergency room physician for observation with a diagnosis of cerebral concussion. A neurosurgical consultation was requested

from Doctor Samuelson. He arrived, but not immediately. It was a full day later that he came to the hospital. His assessment included a comment that no history could be obtained from this restless young male with multiple bruises in light of the patient's condition. Dr. Samuelson affirmed the diagnosis of cerebral concussion and recommended that the boy be held for continued close clinical observation. There was no commentary from him regarding any review of the CAT scan he might have undertaken independently of the radiologist who had reported it. There was no description of any sort of a neurological examination. No history. No neurological examination. No review of the CAT scan. The wrong diagnosis. The wrong treatment. In essence, the perfect prescription for a bad result.

Doctor Samuelson didn't actually need a full medical history from his patient. He didn't even need a detailed account of the hours spent by José in various places under unknown circumstances. Just the comment from his mother that on the day before Samuelson had seen him this boy was not remembering too kindly a person called Rosa would suffice because now José Pollenco was no longer confiding any kind of grievance. He wasn't even talking to anyone, when Doctor Samuelson finally saw him. This very significant change in his condition required interpretation and action on his part. But apparently, Doctor Samuelson didn't consider it important to interview the boy's mother. For that reason there was little prospect he would make any pertinent comments in José's medical record stemming from an awareness of the progression of José's symptoms. It is hard to figure why he would not consider it worth his while to spend whatever time was necessary to telephone this patient's concerned parents both to reassure them and to become knowledgeable of what had been going on with his new patient.

That close and continuous observation was in order was an oddball wisdom. It would be apparent from any perusal of the nursing and the medical records that during the almost twenty-four hours which had already elapsed by the time Doctor Samuelson saw him, José had had already been observed to deteriorate. How much longer did his worsening have to be documented or "observed"? By then such follow-up had already established the incontestable fact that the José who once spoke, no longer did so. Also that he who once thrashed about constantly, now moved only occasionally and then only if disturbed.

After another thirty-six hours of "observation," José suddenly reared up in bed and complained of a "terrible headache." He fell back vomiting. The orthopedic surgeon, on whose service the boy had been admitted as a case of multiple injuries, called for his neurosurgical consultant to come back. No response from Doctor Samuelson. He could not be located. His occasional backup, Doctor Taylor, that same fellow who would later testify in his behalf, was not available either. And then one pupil began to dilate. Granted that consternation over José's condition did at least materialize in that hospital. Handwringing, however, does not ordinarily translate into a reversal of such adverse clinical trends. This was another typical circumstance requiring administration of mannitol and intubation of the patient for oxygenation and hyperventilation. The very much alarmed orthopedic surgeon, a Board certified specialist with practice limited to injuries, and well versed in the principles underlying such treatment did not feel it right, as he saw it, to order what was required by a neurosurgical patient. One might be tempted to say he was frightened out of his depth! And so José would have no recourse but to succumb.

Years later, the family of José Pollenco would find it difficult to find a neurosurgeon willing to testify against Doctor Samuelson. I became the physician who finally agreed to support their claim. After reviewing the hospital records and the sworn statements of the doctors I became so troubled by the degree of negligence that I felt compelled to ring up a professor who had had a hand in training him. I even went so far as to suggest that this professor was really the best person to testify against him. "Forget it! I'm too old. I don't travel anymore, much less do surgery. And I know him personally." Very quickly, he had touched all the usual bases for not getting involved. "Besides, I fired his ass out of my training program at the end of his first year. The son of a bitch never even tried to learn anything. And he was just plain damned lazy. As far as I'm concerned he was, and will always be, an absolute menace!" But mum was his word otherwise.

Samuelson had been clever enough, however, to pick up a year of further training in this country, another in Canada, then back to the states for a final two years, until he had put together enough time to qualify for his specialty board examinations. Over the subsequent years, professional advancement and financial success were the byproducts of his social finesse and political liaisons. As for his clinical acumen? It had already resulted in the biggest number of medical malpractice suits ever to be lodged against a single practitioner in the history of his midwest community. That he was invariably found not guilty was no proof of his skills or knowledge, or that the complaints against him were frivolously lodged. He had been savvy enough to establish his practice in a conservative district, notorious for the confidence of its citizenry in its doctors, for their readiness to stand by them, and for an abiding suspicion of any outsider physicians presuming to intrude with fault-finding accusations. In that jurisdiction such out-of-town experts for a plaintiff were easily characterized by defense lawyers, regardless of the extremity of the medical negligence, as unscrupulous hired guns. It was also suspected by several attorneys who customarily represented injured parties, that Doctor Samuelson even had enough political connection and clout to have certain judges in his pocket.

It was for these reasons that the law firm representing the Pollencos did not seriously expect to prevail. That was the opinion senior members of the firm had reached years in advance of the trial. But there had been no settlement offers, and so the Pollencos' lawyers were obliged to go to court. Their obligation, however, did not extend so far as to assign one of their best or most experienced trial lawyers to the case. They designated a woman attorney who was very good at appreciating the torment of José's parents, and who was also a very sympathetic person. But the practice of law is only concerned with winning cases, not with being nice. Lawyers who win are clever, conniving, or persistent practitioners who ploddingly build their cases upon a persuasive weight of evidence. Or they may appeal to juries by the projection of any number of personal features. Intellectual brilliance, handsome well-groomed appearance, indomitable aggressivity, a commonly acknowledged renown, flamboyance, these are the things that pay off.

This woman attorney was not even used to being in court. Her experience was pretty much limited to work at the office, or in taking the testimony required before trial actually begins, the so-called pre-trial depositions. After only a few hours in court I began to feel that the only chance she might have to win was by the prospect of stirring up resentment among the jurors. Not for what Doctor Samuelson had done to this patient but rather for the many times and ways she herself would seem the victim of abuse by her colleagues, the defense attorneys.

Her performance was pathetic. The objections she raised, and they were few, were usually overruled. Her questions to witnesses on the stand were almost invariably required by the judge to be rephrased upon insistence of the defense team. And she often had difficulties meeting demands of the court because of her lack of trial experience. Almost every time she attacked, she would falter, stand reproved, and then have to move on to some other area of questioning, one more acceptable to the defense. It must have seemed to the jury that she labored on only by the sufferance of opposing counsel. Never, during her opening charges of negligence, was she able, for lack of both tactical skill and a real understanding of her case, to properly address the central issues of the plaintiffs' claim against Doctor Samuelson. And later on, when it was time for her to cross-examine the principal defendant or his expert, she could only smile her way vacuously through a series of off the mark questions which, rather than make some important point or have the effect of feigning the legal prowess she lacked, managed only to provide abundant opportunity for the defendant and his expert to make speeches. This jury would never incline toward a plaintiff's verdict out of sympathy for this woman lawyer, if that was what was being hoped for by the senior partners back at her law firm. And incredibly, that's what I was told when I mentioned to one of them that her poor showing in court was affecting my ability to testify coherently. To the contrary, if those jurors were to have their unbridled way, so impatient were they with her obvious failings as a lawyer, they'd have been more likely to vote her out of that courthouse forever! For three weeks they'd had to sit there, often on the edges of their chairs, straining for her to utter, just once, what obviously had to be said, or to ask what needed to be asked. One can't sympathize with someone who infuriates you.

Moreover, if the jury was at all inclined toward empathy for the deceased patient's mother and father, this lawyer was getting in the way of that also. Emotions are very hierarchal. People do not have it within them to be at the same time both angry and compassionate. And the courtroom antics of the plaintiffs' lawyer angered the jurors. All of this was well appreciated by the attorneys representing Doctor Samuelson, the orthopedic surgeon, and the hospital. For those parties the insurance company had fielded three of their best legal minds. As long as they could manage to keep the jurors resentful of the tedious ineptitude of plaintiffs' counsel, there would be no merciful verdicts for that woman's clients. Injured and bereaved parents could even be shaded as mercenaries; their expert witnesses as inconsistent liars and whores.

The other defense edge, though hardly needed, was the judge. He was an elder jurist scheduled soon to retire and had retreated from any semblance of judicial impartiality. It was clear that his attitude toward Doctor Samuelson was solicitous from the outset, while for Mr. and Mrs. Pollenco his mien was one of overt suspicion. Not that he was discriminating against them in particular. It's just that never in a case of alleged medical malpractice had any jury, once receiving this judge's kind of final instructions, ever returned a verdict for the plaintiff. His bias could be drawn from his record and apparently he had never gone out of his way to appear otherwise. He also managed partiality for the defense by methods other than his judicial rulings or composure. He assumed his easily taken prerogative to make the proceedings as difficult to follow and to schedule as he could. Days in court seemed to end almost as soon as they began. Matters posted to commence at nine-thirty in the morning never started before ten forty-five. His driver would be seen around ten, and a half hour later his query would go out from chambers regarding the general state of readiness to commence. Then, at a quarter to eleven, he would actually assume the bench before a courtroom already crowded and assembled since nine-thirty and the jury would be summoned. Lunch was at noon. Court scheduled to reconvene at one-thirty in the afternoon usually awaited his return until somewhere around two. And there were always the little ten minute recesses presumably out of consideration for the jury, which he could announce at almost any time. At exactly four P.M. the driver reappeared, and no matter what was being argued the judicial gavel fell as indication of the close of another legal day.

When finally it was time for me to go on the stand as plaintiffs' expert what kind of testimony could I manage to give, with that kind of a schedule? I had anticipated no more than a single day of reasonable questioning, divided between the two sides. What I endured was a six day circus of judicial and adversarial flimflam. And it was for that kind of justice, that kind of airing of their grievance, that José's parents had waited six long years to have their day in court. If such justice was "blind," it was only so to the feelings of those who had been injured, who were being injured again, and who had to suffer through it all.

Day after day, the parents were forced to watch the judicial and the defense high jinks. Alternately confused, weeping, or in a rage, they agonized over what was going on. Poorly versed in English, they understood hardly more than that they were losing. Before that judge, or what really amounted to an empty black judicial robe, the nattily dressed defense attorneys were in control of the proceedings. Self satisfied and gloating, with their knowing smiles and derisive laughter, they chided one another over occasional missed opportunities to press even further some deception or misrepresentation of the moment. Then, at day's end, they would strut away triumphantly, devoid of any sensitivity, under the wounded parental gaze, and head off to their local bar. And those two people were not suffering a second time by way of some resurrected ancient grief.

For them, José could never be just a memory. He was with them always as their ever-dying boy. And they were his eternal mourners. Life held nothing for them but their grief. When parents know that a child's death has been unnecessary, there are some who act this way. But now they were raised to a higher level of pain and misery. After six years of almost secluded bereavement they had, at last, made a public appearance to display not only their sorrow, but anger for the doctor they held to be responsible for that death. And yet they were being confronted with what hardly appeared to them, their limited grasp of English notwithstanding, a reasoned, legally couched defense of the detested doctor, but rather a wild and gleeful anticipatory celebration of their impending defeat. By implication, the killing of their child was being justified. Their own lawyer had to spend as much time trying to console them, and to calm them down, as to plead her case. She had no success with either endeavor. Unfortunately, their adversaries in that courtroom seemed to deliberately make her task all the harder by flaunting their disregard for the feelings of that mother and father. It wasn't that any of their legal tactics were that unusual. They adopted the methods, assumed the conventional posture, and followed the customary habits of lawyers. It was how apart from that they carried on as presuming, callous winners that is hard to either understand or forgive. Were they to sport an anticipatory savoring of victory in some tennis game as now they did their case in that courtroom it would not go well for them. They'd be hooted from the field.

Doctor Samuelson claimed to have made hospital rounds and re-examined José on the third day, the fateful one in question. He said he did so only a few hours before the patient's condition deteriorated. He would have it that the next thing he did was to sign out to Doctor Taylor. The patient's neurological status had been no different from what he'd observed on the previous morning. But there was no nursing record of that visit, nor had he made any notation in the patient's chart. In fact there was no hospital record of his having visited any of his other patients in the hospital on that particular day. About not writing anything in José's medical chart, he claimed there was "no need to do so." He only makes notations of significant changes, and as he said, there were none to be recorded. Everything was "rock stable."

There are doctors who make few entries in hospital charts only because they do not understand the importance or appreciate the requirement for doing so. There are others who are too busy or too lazy to bother. Some just occasionally forget. Certain physicians may not know what needs to be written, or how to properly record what should be entered. Insecure, bewildered doctors may be afraid to leave a paper trail which exposes their uncertainty, bafflement, or ignorance. They will not risk the chance of it being found out later that at a particular point in time, when the clinical circumstances called for one line of thinking, they were off on the wrong track, or were possibly on no track at all. But by and large, the ploy most frequently favored for covering up absences, or the unwillingness to commit medical observations or opinions to something written in the record, is the one used by Doctor Samuelson. No news is not news, so why should a busy doctor be expected to spend his or her valuable time penning or dictating endless, so-called meaningless comments, just to pretty up a medical record? It may not matter to such doctors that the accreditation commission for hospitals requires it, particularly in the case of seriously ill patients being seen by consultants. And doctors facing legal charges of negligence see their omission as an advantage because they are confident that few lawyers for an aggrieved patient will ever become familiar with that requirement, or if they should learn about it, they are not likely to be permitted a submission of that conduct code in a court of law as something for a jury to take account of. Even in the improbable circumstance of it happening, juries find it hard to comprehend the concept of a linkage between good medical care and good record keeping. More than one negligent doctor has gotten off insisting that "all of this paperwork is just stuff for the record room, and hasn't anything at all to do with how well I cared for my patient."

Doctor Samuelson had been nowhere near the hospital on that critical day. Nor had he signed out to anyone. He had disappeared. Doctor Taylor did not know that his friend was out of town, and neither his answering service nor his office were under any advisement from the missing Doctor Samuelson.

But if he had actually visited his patient, what might have been his findings and his conclusions? By then it was two full days since the boy had last managed to speak, and if Doctor Samuelson had not understood such drowsiness to be a problem requiring evaluation at the end of one day, perhaps its persistence after a second twenty-four hours would have provoked him to investigate its cause.

To do that he would have needed to order another CAT scan as an emergency. Such a study was finally carried out, a bit later on, when José's condition became terminal, and was interpreted to show severe generalized brain swelling, as well as two bruises or contusions of the brain surface. The swelling was extensive enough for the ventricles of the brain, its fluid containing chambers, to be so compressed they were narrowed down to the point that they appeared in the scan as mere slits. This represented a condition which is usually treatable by the administration of mannitol when the drug is given while the patient is still responding. If mannitol had been given then, José would have probably recovered. The failure to give it later on, when he was comatose, constituted a lost but only very limited second opportunity to save him. But what about the unrealized better chance to have done so? Because much more importantly, the first CAT scan, the one done immediately following his admission to the hospital wasn't normal either. It also showed severe brain swelling and the same two small contusions. The second CAT scan was worse, but the first was bad enough. The radiologist had erred in calling it normal. Possibly, he considered the ventricles to be small because of the patient's age. Children do have smaller ventricles than adults. But these were just too small for that allowance and the swelling of the brain was quite evident. In fact the swelling was severe enough to have squeezed fluid out of other spaces between the various brain lobules which normally contain it. Maybe he was figuring that the failure of those spaces to fill with fluid was due to some kind of imaging fault inherent in the x-ray technique rather than the consequence of their obliteration by pressure. Perhaps, also, he considered that the whitened areas, the undiagnosed "hyperdensities," represented something other than blood in the contusions. More likely, he just plain and simply goofed. It can happen. As for Doctor Samuelson, he never examined the first CAT scan. He simply took the radiologist's word for it that the scan was normal and was on his hurried way. This is a doctor who seems to place great value upon his time. He routinely charges several hundred dollars for consultations such as this one. That is what he billed José's parents for his brief presence. As precious as his time may be to Doctor Samuelson, it did not count for very much as it was expended on José. So much for what was Doctor Samuelson's unrealized and only actual possibility to treat his patient.

The second coming of this neurosurgeon, supposedly transpiring as an unwitnessed, covert visitation, was nothing more than defense fabrication. If the jury should suspect that Doctor Samuelson's claim to it was mere fantasy, that if the truth were to be known, he was nowhere near that hospital for thirty-six hours during which time his patient was deteriorating, and that he had made no provision for coverage by Doctor Taylor, then even in that jurisdiction there might have been an award to the plaintiffs. So Doctor Samuelson came up with the undocumented second examination of the patient. It only had to be argued that if José was in stable condition by Doctor Samuelson's own finding at that time, only a few hours before he took a sudden, unexpected change for the worse, it would have been too late for anyone to be reasonably expected to save him. Death could be made to seem unavoidable. Sudden inalterable untreatable deterioration, coincidental stroke, mysterious post operative decompression paralysis, out of the ordinary anatomy, the strange and unpredictable ways of "mother nature," the uncooperative patient, these are the standard fabric of routine strategies for the defense of incompetent doctors. Lawyers just take their pick of them. And sad to say, most juries are taken in.

They buy such nonsense. Pleadings of that kind find ready acceptance. That's precisely why they are heard so often in courtrooms. Even though like or similar phenomena are almost never described in the medical or scientific literature, in the courtroom they have the ring of authenticity. But this oft recited duplicitous litany, effective as it may be, counts for no more legitimacy than other dissembling legal tactics utilized by lawyers who have no real belief in their causes when they are assigned to defend doctors they'd never consider going to themselves. As some are wont to say, "What the hell! It's a living. It works. And after all it's only a job. That's all."

The first charge against Doctor Samuelson was that of making an inappropriate diagnosis. Could it really have been a simple "cerebral concussion" when José had not been acting appropriately for more than twenty-four hours at the time he saw him? "Well, he might have been on drugs." There were none. He had already been tested for drugs on admission to the hospital and the results were negative. From the witness stand Samuelson floated other speculations. Blood pressure elevation, charted in the record, did not mean a sign to be taken as it ordinarily would in such a situation, a sign of increased intracranial pressure. It meant that the patient was probably thrashing about too much when the nurses took his blood pressure. José was never observed to exhibit such restless activity. And his very slow pulse was "just what you would expect from an athletic, muscular, well toned young male." José was a scrawny little guy who might amble about occasionally, but then only if he couldn't catch a ride. When he wasn't at school, or eyeing girls, he liked to finger his guitar.

Confronted with the first CAT scan, Doctor Samuelson inclined to "go along with the radiologist" who had read it. It was absolutely normal. He admitted that the second one was different, but by then it was "too late to do anything." Too late, too sick, all too unfortunate. "These things do happen and we can't be expected to perform miracles!"

He became emboldened. Perhaps he'd spotted a juror seeming to nod agreement, understanding, sympathy? Or had Samuelson caught a friendly smile from that one's direction?

What else might have encouraged the shift he made all of a sudden from standard tactical nonsense to what amounted to neurosurgical heresy. For this neurosurgeon "didn't believe, anyway, in giving mannitol." He never used the stuff. He was too afraid of its side effects. So even if he had thought José's brain to be swollen, he would not have treated him like that, not at all, "no way!." What he said was incredible! But so to the point for the purpose of our analysis! Here was yet another instance of the biggest lie being the most difficult to contend with. If because of that utterly outrageous statement Doctor Samuelson might now be branded by contrarily and better advised jurors, drawn from his own community, as being utterly out of step with his professional colleagues elsewhere, for them to condemn him like that would be to just about excommunicate him. And harder yet for those jurors, it would mean having to give up too much of the rock solid faith they had always reserved, not only for him, but for other local doctors possibly not too different from him. Samuelson's big lie could work because people who have little else, tend to cling to their faiths or their prejudices, resist learning otherwise, and usually accept whatever is presented to them, within the conditioned fixity and orientation of their frozen attitudes.

Samuelson's speech was neurosurgical heresy because for more than forty years mannitol and a few other so called osmotic diuretics have been the initially preferred and only proven-to-be-effective drugs for increased intracranial pressure of this kind. I tried to make this important point when it came my turn to testify. If by this time the reader has begun to wonder if perhaps I harp too much on the use of mannitol, seeming to make of it a sort of cure-all panacea, that would be an unfortunate interpretation of the drift of my commentary. The truth of the matter is that except for mannitol and hyperventilation, after more than fifty years of trying other measures, these two methods remain all there is by way of nonsurgical techniques for treating increased intracranial pressure expeditiously. Like all drugs, mannitol does have certain restrictions regarding side effects and dosage as well as other limitations. Also, of all the fluid excreted by the kidney after mannitol is given, hardly any of it is actually drawn from the brain. Most of it comes from other tissues of the body. Furthermore, what small amount of water is extracted from the brain is apt to come from normal, rather than the swollen parts affected by the pathological process. Nevertheless, it is only by removing that small amount of fluid from normal brain areas that the intracranial pressure can be lowered and life sustained, while further and more definitive, often surgical, therapeutic measures are taken. Mannitol provides the much needed window of opportunity permitting life saving diagnosis and treatment that would otherwise be denied. It also affords patients with this boy's kind of brain swelling the time needed for it to subside spontaneously. For Doctor Samuelson to claim he didn't believe in mannitol, or that mannitol was too toxic, and so he would not use it, was tantamount to saying he did not believe in saving lives at all.

When you go that far, however, it probably isn't possible to risk your credibility one whit more by boldfaced advocacy of what is totally implausible. So Doctor Samuelson followed up with much the same rejection of giving oxygen, of intubation, of hyperventilation, in so many words, of doing almost anything a reasonably well informed, prudent neurosurgeon would consider appropriate for getting the intracranial pressure down. To intubate José would be to "invite the risks of anaesthesia." Not so. No anaesthesia would have been required. But even if that were the case, would it not be better to assume some risk rather than to simply let the patient die? "Sedation would have to be maintained and it is dangerous under the circumstances of head injury." Again not true. To the contrary, sedation has been advocated in patients controlled by intubation, as a measure for protecting the brain by reducing its metabolic need for oxygen when swelling has limited the availability of oxygen.

And then, more from him about mannitol. "Why it makes the brain shrink. And you wind up taking a big chance of a fatal hemorrhage. I wouldn't want to do that. Not for anything." There was no such risk in this patient. The only risk was that without treatment, as finally happened, a malignant progressive form of brain swelling would spell the end for this patient. Doctor Samuelson was out to alarm the jury and then to recruit it to his cause. No longer was this to be a courtroom. It was to be imagined that they were in a hospital emergency room and that he, Doctor Samuelson, was all that stood between them and the threat of being bled to death by the misguided ministrations of what some plaintiff's expert might propose. And such a risky business was supposed to be better treatment than he had rendered? Rubbish! Shameful!

Bleeding with mannitol can and does occur, but it's uncommon and usually confined to circumstances in which a patient has had an acute arterial hemorrhage from an aneurysm or some other vascular brain abnormality which may rebleed if intracranial pressure is taken down too far. José had no such condition. Nor did Doctor Samuelson confess that even in those clinical situations there can be occasions when mannitol will be used, irrespective of the risk, in order to buy the precious time required for getting patients of that kind ready for surgery. Otherwise, before they can be operated upon to remove a clot resulting from such a hemorrhage, they may expire. These are instances in which because of the bleeding into the brain, and the accumulation of large blood clots, the secondary swelling has become life threatening. José had no blood clot. He had no vascular abnormality. He was at no risk of either bleeding or rebleeding.

Head injuries of the kind from which he suffered present problems of treatment based almost entirely upon the need to treat brain swelling. That is sometimes the particular issue when head injury occurs in young people. As a result of absorption by the brain of the kinetic energies of the blow, its blood vessels malfunction. They expand in size, that is, they dilate. The medical term for that condition is post traumatic vasoparalysis. It is secondary to a compromise of the ability of smooth muscle in the blood vessel wall to contract and thereby to maintain an appropriately sized channel through which blood can pass at the correct speed and in appropriate quantity. By the vessels dilating they come to take up much more room than they would ordinarily. Because the brain and all of its contents, including the blood vessels, are enclosed within a fixed space within the cavity of the skull, the result of even that small increase in the intracranial volume is a rise of pressure within the cranial cavity. It also happens that because the blood vessels are now dilated, and do not vary in caliber as they would normally to limit blood flow, unusually high flow or pressures are passed along through the arteries into thin walled smaller vessels called capillaries. The capillaries are not made to withstand these high levels of pressure. Swelling then occurs, because under such pressure loads, the capillaries leak fluid into the spaces around them. This is known as vasogenic edema. The comprehensive term applied to the problem, which also involves a failure of the arteries to constrict as they would normally to elevations of blood pressure, is loss of cerebral autoregulation. Usually, when a deterioration of this kind follows head injury it is self limited. It will subside after a few days. Successful treatment, however, depends upon using the medical measures already referred to: mannitol, intubation, oxygen and hyperventilation, until natural resolution can take place. But if such treatment is withheld, the patient will usually succumb to some kind of a brain herniation. Because in this situation the swelling is generalized, death is not apt to be from the uncal type of herniation. The pressure does not build up on only one side of the brain, as it did for Leroy or Charles, to cause an uncal herniation. Rather, the whole brain swells and begins to move uniformly downward. As it does so, that part of it at the base of the brain, the tonsils of the cerebellum, come to be pressed against the lower brain stem, the medulla oblongata, site of the respiratory center. This compression occurs within a bony opening in the floor of the skull, the foramen magnum. There is no room in that small passageway for so much brain tissue. For that reason the cerebellar tonsils are called "incarcerated," in other words entrapped or stuck in that position, becoming sometimes also referred to as "strangulated," meaning both entrapped and deprived of blood flow. This causes the cerebellar tissue to break down, become "necrotic," and swell even more against the medulla oblongata. Then, the patient generally stops breathing and the blood pressure falls because life functions of that kind are controlled by the compressed and failing medulla oblongata.

That this was set to happen could have been foreseen. José did develop a slight enlargement of one pupil from a minimal degree of uncal herniation which stabilized and was tolerated. But then, twelve hours later, he progressively herniated the cerebellar tonsils against the medulla and no longer breathed. No one did anything for him when his pupil showed that slight alteration. It was a warning which went ignored.

Doctor Samuelson had no real interventional involvement with his patient. His actual grasp of José's needs was not much more than might be incurred by the hazy awareness that a head-injured lad was present, confined to a bed, and moving only when stimulated. His was a quick hospital walk-through and more a dalliance with diagnostic labelling than any kind of proper clinical evaluation. For reasons never known, he took a full day to show up at the hospital and when he finally did so, seemed to have been in a hurry. Also, contrary to his testimony, he never came back. According to his former professor, he had always been either too quick, or too lazy, or too uninformed, to meet his professional obligations.

What he saw in bed, the one and only time he visited José, was a drowsy battered young male who moved all of his limbs and who protested any painful stimulation. There is no reason to suggest that further detailed examination at that time would have shown much else, although clinical evaluation is usually pushed much further. But there was a question that he needed to pause and seriously consider. Why was this boy still sleeping off the effects of a blow, or of a series of blows to the head, sustained more than twenty four hours before? Only the CAT scan could offer answers to that query. Not to personally examine the CAT scan in order to seek an answer was to take unnecessary chances because any further worsening of his condition would be reflected by clinical signs of the kinds of deterioration that can proceed too fast to allow effective treatment. No competent neurosurgeon, faced with this kind of patient, would ordinarily rely on the interpretation of a CAT scan undertaken by someone else, particularly when that interpretation is rendered by a general radiologist and not a neuroradiologist. There is too much at stake.

Even if a neuroradiologist, that is a radiologist who specializes in CAT scans of the brain and other studies pertaining to neurological diagnosis, had called it normal, the scan would still require prompt viewing by the doctor with the ultimate responsibility for its interpretation, the neurosurgeon undertaking care of the patient. Some note by an intern that a radiologist had considered the CAT scan to be normal should not have served as a basis for final conclusions on the part of Doctor Samuelson. To go on that alone was inappropriate.

What Doctor Samuelson did was assume that this bruised and shaken up youth would eventually come around and do just fine. He had probably chanced it that way with other head injuries and lucked out. Gamblers have the problem, however, of getting used to big bets and risking large losses. So after his cursory examination of José, when Doctor Samuelson disappeared, he was not troubled enough by his high stakes gamble, while he pursued other matters, to give it any further thought. He certainly could not have been thinking much about José, in any caring sense, when it is considered that he advised no one about his going off call, and asked no other neurosurgeon to look in on José during his absence. The next thing he knew about José was that he had expired.

Where do busy doctors go? What pursuits make them hard to find and limit the time they have for patients? Not uncommonly they are involved with matters apart from medicine. Neurosurgeons, as a rule, clear more than five hundred thousand dollars a year. Many earn more than a million. They do that well in spite of having to pay out fifty to one hundred thousand dollars annually for malpractice insurance. With so much money in hand the medical needs of patients may have to wait on the doctor's earliest opportunity to take leave of some non-professional diversion or avocation made possible by all of that wealth.

For neurosurgeons, the good life abounds. There can be every conceivable recreational pursuit and others the ordinary person might not even dream of. The opportunities to indulge one's whims extend from high flying travel and appreciation of the arts, to operatic singing lessons and premature exhaustion from drugs and alcohol. Investments and other business pursuits commonly make demands upon time better focused on medical concerns. When there is so much disposable income, and doctors are away either because of it or the rigors of their medical practices, it is no oddity, either, that the families of physicians may come to have unusual problems, causing further distraction from medical matters. There is certainly no law against a man, like one I know, starting out as a neurosurgeon and winding up with more than five hundred million dollars, his own hospital, extensive real estate holdings and three families to support. But there should probably be one requiring him to be around when his patient needs him and to concentrate on that patient's problem.

For what professional services is all of this money earned? In neurosurgery, the answer to such a question is easily come by. There have been surveys of the numbers and kinds of operations performed by neurosurgeons. A common neurosurgical procedure is the placement of a bypass shunt for hydrocephalus, an enlargement of the fluid containing ventricular system when under pressure from some kind of absorptive interference or obstruction. A shunt is just a little plastic tube passed under the skin to connect the ventricle of the brain to some other body cavity. The operation is done when the fluid formed in the ventricular system cannot be reabsorbed within the brain and has to be provided some other place for its absorption. There are several clinical conditions requiring such treatment. The operation is very simple. A neurosurgeon learns how to do it in his first year of training. He doesn't even have to see the brain when he does the procedure. Usually, only a small "burr" hole is made in the skull and a one inch incision or puncture permits access to the abdominal cavity. For this service the neurosurgeon will charge anywhere from one to three or more thousand dollars. Another commonly performed neurosurgical operation is revision of the shunt because in most cases it doesn't work for very long. It gets plugged up. That is not to say this kind of surgery is unimportant. Without it the patient will grow gradually worse. It is to say, however, that the operation is commonplace, takes little time, is no measure of any high degree of skill, is unreasonably priced for what's involved, and constitutes a very lucrative way for a surgeon to spend his time.

What next? It is an operation in the low back or neck, often unnecessarily performed, for a "slipped" intervertebral disc. Not usually necessary because, when these operations are performed, it is generally much too soon. If neurosurgeons would just wait a few weeks, the symptoms would subside more than ninety percent of the time. But then they would not earn two to four thousand dollars for removing the offending disc. Such operations are also not very demanding in respect of the technical skills required for their performance. Quite a few neurosurgeons do hardly anything other than disc surgery.

The rest of the time spent by neurosurgeons in the operating room is for the occasional brain tumor, usually malignant and not very treatable surgically, or for the evacuation of blood clots secondary to head injury. Only infrequently does the average neurosurgeon have to deal with a demanding situation requiring high levels of surgical skill or dexterity, as in operations upon deeply placed benign tumors of the brain, or in placing clips upon bleeding aneurysms or vascular malformations. It's hard to understand the cultivated awe we have for "brain" surgeons other than as some kind of clever self promotion scheme. Rocket scientists also?

The problem arises, consequently, that the neurosurgeon may become so busy running from hospital to hospital or office to office to veritably beat the bushes for candidates for operation, necessary or not, or is so much away on nonmedical pursuits, that often when really needed, this specialist is not to be found. And that is true even when the neurosurgeon works in a group practice where someone is always supposed to be on call. It was recently reported in a respected medical journal that if you break your neck in the United States, about forty-six percent of the time you cannot manage to be seen by a neurosurgeon during the first forty-eight hours of hospitalization. Cry for us all!

José did not have a broken neck. He had brain swelling. But it was par for the course that for his different kind of urgent need he also lacked the prompt and undivided attention of one of these affluent fellows. What he got was a peripatetic doctor, late to arrive and quick to be off again to somewhere else. An unreliable fellow who called himself a neurosurgeon. Doctor Samuelson had conducted himself like that for years.

For seven hours the resident doctors, the orthopedic surgeon, the nurses, and the hospital director vainly searched out the whereabouts of Doctor Samuelson. The one pupil remained slightly dilated. José was no longer responding very well to painful stimulation and yet no doctor was moved enough by those findings to order mannitol or to implement an intubation. After six hours they had summoned the other neurosurgeon, Doctor Taylor. At first unavailable also, he finally arrived in keeping with his own schedule, but at precisely the moment José expired secondary to a respiratory arrest. During the subsequent trial, an issue would be made of the fact that at this moment, just before he stopped breathing, José vomited.

"That's why he really died," swore Doctor Samuelson. "He vomited, aspirated his vomitus, and began to choke, thereby elevating the pressure in his head. That's how he came to have tonsillar herniation. It was just one of those sudden, unpredictable things that no one can foretell or ever hope to treat." No matter that on autopsy, examination of the lungs failed to show any evidence of such an aspiration. That absence did not deter Doctor Taylor either, in his turn, from coming to the same conclusion as Doctor Samuelson. And after all, would he not know best? He was there when the patient died, on the very scene- He had observed the vomitus! His opinion, by some queer logic, was supposed to have more coin than anyone else's, even that of the pathologist who had looked at the lung under a microscope and found no signs of an aspiration. And certainly more than that of the plaintiffs' expert, now coming along so many years later. But that Taylor had ever really seen was a dead boy who in the throes of dying, had vomited.

The other findings on postmortem pathological examination, those observed in the brain, never came to the attention of the jury in ways that could sway them. For example, the severe brain swelling that had gone untreated, the real cause of José's death, was never even demonstrated to them by a pathologist.

There have been studies made of malpractice trials in which the inability of juries to find for the plaintiff is beyond comprehension. In one such instance, with which I'm familiar, a neurosurgeon treating a fifteen-year-old boy with a fractured neck following an auto collision, wired up his cervical spine in a manner that paralyzed him. He passed the wires directly through the youth's spinal cord, not only at one but at three different vertebral levels. Those wires were only supposed to stabilize the spine by going through or around bone. They shouldn't have gone anywhere near the spinal cord. The surgeon did nothing further for his paralyzed, previously normal patient other than to ship him out to a rehabilitation center one week after the operation. In another few days, that's where he died. The jurors let the doctor off saying they could not find it in their hearts to convict him. After all, he had not intended, as one of them put it, "to hurt the boy on purpose." The attorney representing the deceased had even had the boy's body exhumed so that the neck could be x-rayed and dissected. Those jurors saw not only x-rays and photographs, they had the actual spinal cord placed before them with the wires sticking out of it. Still, they voted for that doctor. Would they have wanted this to have happened to them? After all, it was their town, their hospital, and their neurosurgeon. They could wind up in a car crash on that very same road. Such questions seem to ring no bells, stir no indignation. The devotion to doctors can be that strong.

There is difficulty enough when seemingly straightforward issues of that sort are presented to juries. The possibility of justice being served becomes even more remote when the medical issues are complex and, as in this case, there are three lawyers for the defense who are masters at obfuscation, a plaintiff's attorney well meaning but inexperienced, a defendant doctor and his expert steadfastly rejecting universally accepted treatments the while aping war heroes, and a prejudiced judge. So finally, it must fall to an expert retained by the plaintiff to persuade the jury.

I did what I could under these trying circumstances. But what good are medical facts which should be persuasive when they can't be gotten across in any ordered, logical, sequence; when each attempt at their presentation becomes obscured by interminable objections from defense attorneys and clumsily put responses from a meek woman lawyer struggling vainly to protect the rights of the deceased? When she would return from arguments before the bench, she had the habit always, of smiling! What could she possibly be smiling about? Each and every time she argued her point of law, she lost! And she was so put upon to argue almost interminably that the proceedings became disorienting, making it near impossible for anyone to draw a cohesive concept of what was happening in that courtroom. The trial lumbered along like this amid an incomprehensible staccato of interrupted assertions, half-said rebuttals, and unrelenting objections. No issues or positions put forth by the plaintiffs were allowed to be explained, and every time Mrs. Coello, the plaintiffs' lawyer, made an effort to do so, they wound up aborted. All that she ever seemed to manage were eternally uttered offerings to "move on to the next subject." These, invariably, were doomed to the same fate as all the others.

If when I testified I could only have given my opinion without interruption, I would have been off that witness stand and gone in less than three or four hours. But that was not permitted under the law. Justice required that I spend six days in court, of which perhaps two were devoted to hearing questions put to me, and of those I was permitted to answer only a few that were actually pertinent. Most of my time was spent waiting for the judge to appear, pacing the courthouse corridors, or when so ordered, standing in a distant corner like an outcast dunce while long winded procedural arguments before the bench required that I be out of earshot of them.

Anytime that Mrs. Coello somehow managed to come up with a question that was properly phrased, not leading in character, consistent with the complaint, and relevant to the issues at trial, there was pandemonium. All three defense lawyers would jump to their feet in unison and object. Then, once again, I had to leave the witness stand and go numbly to my station in a corner while still more arguments were made before the judge. It did not count for very much even if that particular question was finally allowed and I could give my answer. How can jurors even hope to remember what has been asked, or what was the temporarily tabled issue, when the answer doesn't surface until long after seemingly interminable arguments before the judge are finally resolved? Sometimes it was an especially protracted interval. Lawyers don't just argue or object. Theirs is rarely a simple protest. They spend inordinate time giving the elaborate legal grounds for their objections. They put legal precedents before the court to support their contentions. And the judge may have to freshen his memory for such precedents. Which means he declares a recess, goes back to his chambers to study the issue, and everybody awaits his return from deliberating. This judge made very few rulings without such review. He did not seem to know the law well enough for that. If I were to know my medicine no better than that judge knew the relevant law, I would have had to have my medical books open before me almost every time I treated or operated upon a patient.

This kind of incomplete, fragmented, testimony was incomprehensible to those jurors. When they left for home each evening, if they should have happened to reflect upon the proceedings of the day and try to unscramble all of that medical and legal jargon, their recollections could not possibly stand for anything more than the spectacle of a confusingly tedious and tumultuous furor. Their ultimate verdict, therefore, could not rest upon anything other than their gut feelings or personal preferences. It is possible in a courtroom for a physician to teach ordinary people who know no medicine enough of the basic principles to come to rational conclusions. Some doctors manage to do it every day so that patients can make the appropriate decisions regarding their treatment. But you can't teach anyone anything when the courtroom is a clamorous three ring circus and that was what the defense lawyers had determined to make of it.

Also probably fundamental to the defense strategy was what had the appearance of a scheme to keep me on the witness stand forever. After a certain number of days spent enduring this kind of exasperating nonsense, all any reasonable person would want would be to get from that courtroom to an airport and out of there! An academic neurosurgeon like myself is too busy to be delinquent indefinitely in all his other obligations so as to meet what portends to be an open-ended obligation to sit or to pace back and forth endlessly in some courthouse, and then to bed down day after trying day in a neighboring motel a thousand miles away from home. As a university professor I had classes to teach, clinics to run, ongoing research, as well as my own patients who might need me. After awhile, one could just about be tricked into saying anything so burdensome was it to remain in that courthouse. One needs the patience of Job to maintain one's composure and the appearance of objectivity when testifying under such harassment.

For reasons unclear to me, it is considered essential, however, that an expert medical witness not be provoked to a posture of advocacy in support of a plaintiff's case. A doctor is said to risk his credibility if he holds forth vigorously, emotionally, in the delivery of his opinion. Rather, he is expected to calmly, matter of factly, answer the questions. He should be above provocation. So the defense calculated to stir my ire by every means possible. But what is more deserving of advocacy than the truth as one sees it? What can be more befitting of strong and emotionally expressed avowal? And what could be more exasperating than the lawyerly saboteurs in that courtroom who would not ordinarily be held to the issue of truth, and who if they did stumble upon it were not likely to want it within their grasp?

For sure the only ones there sworn to the truth were those who testified. Lawyers are only obliged to win, not to be truthful. The judge does no more than see to it that if they win, it's by the rules. And the rules have nothing whatsoever to do with truth. The rules, moreover, are merely what happens to be the legal vogue of the day. And, they're always changing.

The truth? Behind this boy's death? I'm sure that I was on to it. And the victimization of his parents in that courtroom? It was easily read in the eyes of José's sad faced mother and father.

And even if, because of defense tactics, the medical truths could never be presented in a meaningful way to this jury, then the expert, by ordinarily held understandings, was still supposed to give no indication of his frustration or displeasure. Would it not seem that such a boycott of reasonableness must necessarily subvert the underpinnings of justice? What was happening in that place called for indignant, raging protestation. Not only over medical science turned topsy-turvy, but to give the only feasible signal of that selfsame justice being made a mockery of. And yet, however so inclined, I could not permit himself to explode. I endured the requirements and the restrictions placed upon my testimony by the protocol prescribed for such proceedings. It was all wrong, unnaturally and indecently wrong.

So it happened that for all the days I spent in court the jurors derived no more than some ill-formed, unelaborated idea that in my opinion José's condition of brain swelling required earlier recognition and treatment, preferably with mannitol. Any time that I attempted to give the reasons for my opinions, they were successfully blocked by the defense as "mere speculation" on my part and not "attributable to the condition of José" as otherwise recorded. If all that a jury may consider is opinion, unsupported by the persuasive power of the reasoning behind it, then it is likely to yield to some sympathy or prejudice. And in this case that could only be for what was familiar and neighborly, not for what some outsider expert had to say or for these seemingly hysterical parents appearing more comfortable to speak in Spanish than in a good old Michigan kind of American English. Not only was a bareboned, unreasoned presentation all that I could accomplish during my direct examination, it also happened that cross examination was damaging to my credibility.

Did I or did I not "remember having testified previously" on such and such date, in such and such place, on the matter of somebody versus someone else? I did. And did I recall "having been asked on that occasion" a particular question? Which was then read, as well as the answer I had priorly given. I understood, as soon as I heard the reading of those portions of my earlier testimony, that unless the answer given to that question on this other occasion could be read in its entirety and without editing, along with an essential explanation, it would seem to run counter to the opinion I was rendering now. It would look like my current testimony stood impeached.

There was to be no opportunity to explain. Yes, I surely remembered that testimony but. . . "The question calls for a yes or no answer" droned Samuelson's lawyer over and over. And notwithstanding the objection of the ever smiling Mrs. Coello, the judge agreed. In some other court, an expert would probably have been allowed to explain his answer, but not in this one. Even much later, during her redirect examination of me and after the damage had been done, Mrs. Coello could not manage to meet the legal requirements of that judge for extracting the much needed explanation.

The jurors had been led to believe that I was inconsistent. Therefore, by implication, none of my testimony should be relied upon. In matters of the law, all of a person's statements, past and present, are to be best regarded for their orderliness, their correspondence, and their definitiveness. There is no leeway. There are no shades of gray. And what might be the case in one instance should be expected to apply in another. No matter that my seeming inconsistency was not actual, that it was only made to look so. Doubt, reasonable doubt, of my credibility had been raised. Jurors need and are encouraged to want certainty. For certainty is single minded. It doesn't hesitate. And it's ever ready to vote. The law is just about practiced like a religion that votes, that is adamant in much the same fashion. As for some there can be only one God, so there can be only one truth. For all of its pretenses of logic and soundness, the law can wind up a thoroughly irrational business.

The jury had been clued throughout the trial by overt displays emanating from the defense table to suggest that things were going their way. What could be right about my testimony if it was an obvious delight to the defendants and all of their lawyers? So even when I was contradicting Doctor Samuelson, the strategy was to seem pleased with whatever I said. These were masters of the technique. They had learned well to smile when they heard answers they liked, and to smile even more at answers they probably couldn't bear to hear. There are jurors who have so much difficulty comprehending technical matters they actually formulate final opinions based upon how things appear to be received by the defendants and their lawyers. If just one or two jurors can be hoodwinked that way, a plaintiff's case will be lost.

It happened now that opposing counsel celebrated even more openly my seemingly inconsistent testimony. I had stated in another courtroom on the prior occasion that, as a rule, CAT scans performed following administration of mannitol will show no real reduction in the degree of swelling in those parts of the brain that are injured. Everyone at the defense table had grinned. If only a few months ago, this hired gun was out there swearing up and down that mannitol doesn't do anything for brain swelling, how could he possibly argue the opposite point of view now? Was not his testimony impeached? Here he was, swearing up and down how important it had been to give José this wonder drug, this mannitol, and not that long ago he was opining that the swelling, the edema, would still be there, and you could even see it in a CAT scan as much as a day after mannitol had been given. Not one iota of change in the cerebral edema! And that's how José's life was to have been saved? Ridiculous! This case should be dismissed!

Well, not exactly. Not exactly at all if only Mrs. Coello could get to draw the required explanation from her witness. She was unable to do so. She could not manage it in her pleading to the judge of an expert witness's right to explain his answers fully. Nor could she manage it during her redirect examination of me after my presumably damaging cross examination by the defense. The woman was not able to ask questions in ways satisfactory to the court which allowed me to either elaborate upon my prior answers or to refute their purported inconsistency with what I was saying now. The jury never got to hear that the benefit of mannitol in patients with brain swelling, or in any other condition which raises the intracranial pressure, has nothing at all to do with removal of fluid from the diseased or edematous parts of the brain. The brain fluid that is excreted by the kidneys after the giving of mannitol comes mainly from the normal, not the damaged parts of the brain as I've already described. But what difference does it make as long as the patient gets better by the lowering of intracranial pressure? In a case like this one, if it can be kept down long enough by removal of fluid anywhere in the brain, the edema will eventually subside on its own. The goal is only to get the pressure down. It is not the edema but the raised intracranial pressure produced by it which is life threatening because that pressure reduces blood flow to the brain and may also bring on just the kind of tonsillar herniation as eventually occurred here. CAT scans, invariably, continue to show the swelling, and in certain other disease processes, the abnormalities which have caused it as well, until those abnormalities come under some kind of interventional control. Such a simple thing to get across. But even in her final pleading to the jury, at the time of her summation of the case, when she was entirely uninterrupted, unchallenged, and free to make these critical assertions on her own, Mrs. Coello could not manage it. What can be achieved if the lawyer herself does not understand the medical intricacies and facts, and her expert witness never gets to voice them either? Then there is no trying of the issues. It all comes down to whichever side has the most bluster and trickery and the leanings, but not the reasoning of the jury. Everyone might just as well have stayed home.

Before the final summations, the coroner who had performed the post-mortem examination was called to the witness stand. In addition to a marked swelling of the brain, he had identified the two small areas of contusion, those bruises upon the surface of the temporal and frontal lobes of the left side which I had noted to be present in the CAT scans. His other finding was that of the cerebellar tonsillar herniation which caused the fatal brain stem compression. About the second set of findings, Doctor Taylor, the defense expert, had nothing to say. Why would he? After all, their effects were preventable by treatment. There had been ample opportunity for treatment and there hadn't been any. The contusions, however, were his grounds for a long discourse. He did not take them for the insignificant injuries of the brain surface that I had held them to be. No! Far from it! Albeit inconsiderable in size, in his opinion, they stood to produce major neurological handicaps for José, should he have somehow managed to survive. This patient, by their effects, would most certainly have been paralyzed over his right side and unable to speak. He would have been "aphasic." He omitted to mention that, when aroused, José, in spite of those bruises, did in fact speak quite well, until finally becoming stuporous. No recall, either, by Doctor Taylor that José always moved all four of his limbs without any difficulty. Those contusions were at the tips of the brain where there are no functions whatsoever for either movement of the limbs or speech. Doctor Taylor was lief to say whatever he wanted. After all, this was not medical school where you can be flunked out if you spout such utter drivel. And this was not a medical conference where colleagues would consider you bereft of your senses for that kind of foolishness. This was only a courtroom, where the defense expert, although also sworn to tell the truth, often takes every liberty. In a courtroom anything and everything, goes. There is much being said about the conspiracy of silence operating in medicine, that disposition of physicians to look the other way, refusing either comment or action regarding medical negligence. But what about their other conspiracy, the one to misrepresent basic medical teaching, even scientific facts, so that doctors can get away with malpractice and have their injured patients go uncompensated? Members of the medical profession promise no cures but not uncommonly some of them offer at least one bizarre warrantee. They will try to do whatever is required to get a colleague off the hook.

In what other walk of life is there so much security? Just to graduate from medical school is to have a certain measure of success guaranteed. You should not even flounder after that. And if because of you, some patient like José should suffer, it doesn't matter how flawed your treatment may have been, there's always some kind of doctor out there who can be recruited to defend you. In other occupations, people just fail. They lose their jobs, their homes, businesses. They go bankrupt. They often stand rejected. Only in the practice of medicine does everyone find a way to succeed. I know of one untalented fellow who got through medical school only because his brother was president of the university. He was never able to pass the licensing examination of any state in the country. But even he managed to find a way to see patients and to prosper. First in the navy and later on as a hospital employee. So when Doctor Samuelson was sued, he was not concerned enough about it to even show up in court very often. He'd make out, guilty or not guilty. As for being present to at least make a show of indignation over being charged with medical negligence, he did as much, but for the most part, only by his lawyer's insistence. If he'd have had his own way, he'd have stayed away. He had no doubts whatever that he'd prevail. And he could count on this particular jury to even resent their doctor having had charges pressed gainst him.

Samuelson's few appearances were reserved for times when I was on the witness stand criticizing his care of José. During my oft interrupted testimony he was prone to shake his head over what was being said. Throughout his show of what was made to seem a flabbergasted disagreement with my testimony his gaze would always search for eye contact with the jurors, occasionally managing to lock on to one of them, so as to attempt a silent influence, or to project his wordless disparagement of the worth of what I happened to be saying. These conspiratorial eyeings of the jurors were a way, also, of signalling them as to his protestation of the irresponsible lack of restraint and candor on my part, and the unfairness of the effort being made to denigrate him and to deceive them. Then he would smile, so as to beam his confidence in them, and his satisfaction, otherwise, for the way his trial was going. The jurors were to sense his gratitude for any inclination they might already have to exonerate him.

Usually, his departures from court took place in ways contrived to divert the attention of the jurors away from the witness stand and toward his own exaggerated posturing. These leave takings were associated, invariably, with the exchange of knowing nods between him and his attorney, as well as bestowal upon that one of a certain amount of congratulatory back pounding delivered in his manly, upstanding, and righteous way. Good job! Good job! And so again, most obviously, was it not going badly for the plaintiffs and their professorial co-conspirator? He could convey all of that in open court without uttering a single word!

During the final day of plaintiffs' case, confident he would win out because of the inability of opposing counsel to present a coherent argument against him, Doctor Samuelson decided upon a magnanimous show of sympathy for José's parents. He would not be one to harbor a grudge. They could be reconciled. On the courthouse steps he made his approach. "I'd like you to try, just try some little bit to understand," urged this good-hearted fellow. "There was no way to save José. There was nothing, absolutely nothing that I or anyone else could do. Please try to believe me in this. And there was no way either, that anybody could know it was about to happen, that we were about to lose him. So for God's sake at least make an effort to forget all of this. Get it behind you! Get on with your lives! Start thinking about all your other children. Think about what you're doing to them with all this grief and pent up hatred you've had for me. It's just not reasonable to keep carrying on like this."

They were stunned. But not by what he'd said. They didn't catch a single word of it. All communication between them, the court, and even their lawyer had required the help of an interpreter. They could barely understand a few words of English. Rather, they were shocked by the affront of this terrible man, their child's murderer, to so much as address them, to come that close, to violate a space between them that should never be so fouled. The father, as always, since the death of his son, and by the measure of his wife's perpetual grieving, was a man drained gray and incapable of lively expression. To grasp his hand was to feel the numbing cold immediacy of his child's grave. The mother, however, was possessed of a mean-tempered, simmering fury which never abated. She, like her husband, existed solely for the memory of her son, but her world was no more than a place of maledictions, and for a single person. "Assassin! Assassin!" She lunged for Samuelson's face. He was lucky. If a little less nimble, or without the quick reaction of his lawyer, who pulled him aside, he would have gone down under her.

She may have been helped in some small measure by the catharsis of this outburst after so many years of embattled waiting. There would not be any other opportunity, or any other way, for her to get at Doctor Samuelson. A little of his skin under her nails, a few scratches on his face, at least now there was that much pain for him also! Why should she and her husband be the only ones to suffer? This horrible doctor, responsible for all of their torment, was he not ever to be punished? So much agony!

Anyone under the delusion that all strong feelings eventually peter out should bear witness to these two people. They have wounds of the spirit which time will never heal. And because they nurture an anger forever denied its target, it will have whatever it can. It will have them. That anger and their pain is beyond the reach of rational argument. It also rebukes the well meaning but futile gestures of solace. It is too charged up for that. And it is theirs to the death. That is the price paid for our being civilized, for adjudicating our differences, instead of taking revenge in the old ways. It is also the price paid by all the other members of that family for one irresponsible doctor's neglect.

Doctor Samuelson was careful, thereafter, to keep his distance from the Pollencos. During subsequent presentation of testimony in his defense, if he chose to appear, he would first turn a wary eye in their direction. Someone commented that he even worried if their feelings would be more inflamed should they in some way comprehend everything being said in that courtroom. Particularly that part of it which extolled his virtues as a conscientious, high minded physician, well thought of by the community, his medical peers, and a multitude of grateful patients. It's hard to fully accept another person's inability to comprehend one's own language. There is always the suspicion of their being, at least to some extent, able to understand. Apparently he worried about the possibility of that, of their having so much as a hunch about how the jury was being conned. Would some vague hint of what was happening propel the mother again, right across the courtroom, or a hallway, in his direction? They understood, of course, none of those words being spoken. They knew, from an interpreter, only that now it was the defense's turn. And for them, what possibly could be the worth of anything said by or about this doctor, or of the treatment he had given their boy? They had a settled opinion on that and also upon the amount of hatred due this Samuelson. It could hardly be exceeded. But any outburst from them could only be under his own provocation, as had already happened. Just let him steer clear of them, not suffer them again the insult of his close presence! As boldly and as self-righteously as Samuelson flaunted his manner before the court, he knew enough from that earlier experience to take pains to step well around those two people.

Thus it was that during the deliberations of the jury, Doctor Samuelson was nowhere to be seen around the courthouse. The attorneys who had defended him, however, had no particular regard or concern for the feelings of the parents. They loitered there, hanging around, making the most of their privilege in that respect stemming from their position as officers of the court. They did not have to stay, and to carry on as they did, but it was the usual way for these particularly insensitive lawyers. Appreciating that the parents' fundamental focus of resentment was the doctor, and not them, they made merry of their waiting while just a few feet away the glum mother and father of the dead boy anticipated, by the advisement of their own lawyer, the very worst. It would never occur to these defense attorneys that to a non-involved but perceptive and knowledgeable spectator their antics might seem even more offensive than those of their client. They had managed legally, but nevertheless unscrupulously, to compromise justice, and now they were set to openly celebrate the result of their labors before those disadvantaged by them. Is there another animal which parades its defeat of the vanquished? Which abuses the overwhelmed?

So when the jury announced for the defendant, the parents groaned and wept, but the defense lawyers exited directly past them into a bright spring afternoon, laughing as they went, over the good looks and shapely legs of young women passing. Then they took off to their favored local bar where they were awaited by the doctors already toasting one another.

7

Rosana and Luis

STANDARD

Doctors in residency training programs must be closely super-vised by fully qualified attending physicians not only in operat-ing rooms but for all of their decision making. They should not work independently before completing their training programs. The occurrence of untreated epilepsy is not grounds for operating upon a vascular malformation of the brain in a middle aged or older patient particularly when the malformation is large or lo-cated on the left side.

What might an Italian girl of nineteen and a fifty-eight-year old Puerto Rican truck driver have in common? A vascular malformation of the brain, and doctors who would operate for no purpose other than to en-hance their skills.

She was fair and lively, laboring away in a small west side factory sewing in the linings of men's jackets. Another of many immigrants to make her way without speaking the language. When she began to have convulsions, the doctor in a neighbor-hood health clinic handed her small white capsules that were red banded, to be taken three times a day: dilantin. He gave her the medication and held up three fingers. Thinking that to mean for three days, on the fourth, because of her misunderstanding and his flawed way of communicating, she stopped taking whatever unestablished amount she had been swallowing, had several more convulsions, and was carried off by ambulance from the factory to a university hospital. It was her fate to be studied there by many kinds of specialists bent only on single

mindedly addressing the cause of her epileptic attacks and not
her ordinary medical needs.

When the doctors asked permission to operate, exactly what
she was told is not known. But what could have been her terrible imperative to agree to so formidable a surgical procedure?
And to that end, was she misled? Although it would be later
insisted that she had benefit of a full explanation, not even a
hint of one is conveyed by the hospital chart. There is only the
routine, nonspecific, signed and duly witnessed consent for
surgery and the x-ray report of abnormal blood vessels, what is
called a vascular malformation, in the parietal lobe of the left
side of her brain.

You certainly couldn't tell from any routine physical examination that there existed such a problem, unless one listened with a stethoscope applied to the left side of her head.
Then, a skilled examiner would hear the soft swishing sound of
blood passing directly from arteries to veins, instead of going
through the usually intervening smaller vessels known as capillaries. This normal and more conventional, passage of blood
is completely silent. Rosana heard no noise at all. It was audible
only to the doctors. And they determined to quiet it by removing the thing which was causing the sound. All she knew was
that on three different occasions she had fainted. There is also
nothing to suggest her ever being informed that the same medication she had taken so haphazardly, if swallowed faithfully on
a daily basis, would probably have prevented any further convulsions. Or, in any event, that an operation would hardly be
likely to cure her of them.

Her parents had no better understanding of what affected
their beautiful and only daughter. They sat at her bedside, wide-
eyed and disbelieving, intimidated by the complex paraphernal-
lia of a major teaching hospital. Plain folk from a little village
in Sicily, who would they be to know as much or better than the
multitude of smartly dressed young doctors in their long white
coats, always scurrying about with so many different instruments amidst all of those blinking and chattering machines.
Surely, they must be dedicated only to the rigors of saving
lives. Like their daughter, the parents spoke no English. Per-

haps, if they had witnessed certain other machines, the ones operated by doctors and nurses who labor after the fact of operation in recovery rooms and intensive care units, they would have had some second thoughts. Machines are not so reassuring, so seemingly boastful, when attached to patients who move and breathe no longer on their own.

Vascular malformations, also known as arteriovenous anomalies of the brain, are congenital, which means that they are there from birth. They consist of defective tissues resulting from a failure of certain blood vessels of the brain to develop normally and they vary in size and location, tending over time to grow larger, but only slowly. Symptoms may occur at any age, but the general tendency is for them to first develop in youth or early adulthood. Patients can experience convulsions, intracranial bleeding, strange machinery-like noises, or progressive impairment of one or more specific brain functions. There can be problems with speech, limb movements, sensation, or vision. These so called neurological deficits occur infrequently and only after many years of enlargement of a limited number of such malformations. On the basis of the best information available, the only thing that can be predicted with regard to hemorrhage is that there is about a one percent chance of recurrent bleeding during any year subsequent to a first hemorrhage. A bleed of this kind carries about a ten percent risk of death. No one knows what chance, if any, there may be of hemorrhage in a patient who has never bled, and there is nothing to suggest that patients who have seizures have any greater tendency to bleed than those who do not have seizures. Some correlation exists between the size of a malformation and the possibility of a bleed. Smaller malformations and those more deeply situated in the brain seem to bleed a bit more frequently than those which are large and superficial.

More definite, in many ways, than the unpredictable natural course of this disease is the result of operation. For the moderate to larger sized malformations, attempts at complete surgical excision are associated with a mortality of ten percent or more. Serious neurological complication and disability generally runs even higher among patients who manage to survive surgery. Operations do not provide relief from epileptic seizures. In fact, after an operation, convulsions may appear for the first time among patients never subject to them before. Such a complication of surgery is the result of postoperative scarring, which always takes place, and is not preventable. Surgery is generally avoided except in patients with a history of recurrent hemorrhage or progressive disabling neurological deficit, who have vascular malformations of small size that are also favorably situated for removal. They should not be located so that any surgical attack upon them, because of their involvement of vital brain areas, would impose a certainty of unacceptable disability or high risk of death. Rarely, during childhood, small, incidentally discovered malformations are removed from regions of the brain that can be entered quite safely. Surgery isn't performed to prevent convulsions that have never been treated medically.

These are the relevant facts, the governing principles of treatment, and the statistics. Admittedly, there are always questions to be raised about statistics. The difficulties, however, do not generally derive from data. Figures do not lie. But there are individuals with an undisclosed agenda who know what to do with figures. They will misrepresent them. And there are also those who will pay no attention to them at all. Hardly is it possible to say which of these is the greater dereliction. Either is bad enough. But worst by far, however, is insistence that something is the case for which there is no data at all. These two patients, with the same disease, but otherwise so dissimilar, had that in common. They were frightened into surgery by being told they were the carriers of "time bombs, time bombs in their heads." Without an operation, an immediate operation, they would die from hemorrhage. And "that bomb might explode at any moment." What induced them to be operated upon was the presentation not of fact, but of poppycock. And the motive for it, both times, was a self-promoting one. Two lives were put at extreme risk, with no possibility of benefit for either patient; and yet the neurosurgeons who carried out these operations hardly came to learn very much or to become better operators for their performance of them.

If an elapse of time had Rosana at risk, it was not by the threatening imminence of a damaging hemorrhage from her vascular malformation. It stemmed, if the truth were to be known, from the need to avoid a deadline, but not that kind, or any other having to do with her medical needs. The Tuesday following her hospital admission was simply the next available day in the operating room allotted to neurosurgical scheduling, and it was precariously close on to being too late if the time was not requested. That slot in the schedule, one ordinarily taken by the neurosurgical department, would have to be relinquished to some other surgical service if it was not spoken for. Rather than lose the time available to them, the neurosurgeons reserved it for Rosana. They could always, later on if need be, work a substitution with some other neurosurgical patient and cancel her operation. But scheduled events in medicine have often a tenacity and momentum of their own. And so it was not by any serious reasoning that she happened to be posted for surgery; it was rather the consequence of this strategy to hold on to a time slot. Things were slow on neurosurgery, Rosana happened to be there, and if a department starts to forego the time assigned it for operating, someone may choose to review that service's actual need of the operating time relegated to it. Anyway, by the day scheduled for her, there was always the chance that Rosana might actually prove to be an appropriate candidate for surgery. It was deemed a good idea, therefore, to expedite, that is rush along, her work-up. In the space of a mere three days, the vascular malformation, diagnosed previously by CAT scan, was also visualized in radioisotopic studies, cerebral arteriograms, and a magnetic resonance imaging procedure (MRI).

The lure of such a vascularity can grow more and more intense by a kind of enticement related to something other than the marvelous image enhancements and exaggerations made feasible by all of this new technology. The repetitive demonstrations of grotesqueries of human anatomy, by their very frequency and variety, have a peculiar way of tantalizing and provoking their beholders. And then it may happen that some surgeons for whom to live is to operate, and for whom to operate is the only way to live, may take these transfigurations of normality to be both objectionable and a challenge to their surgical skills. They respond not with objective deliberation, but with emotion and action. It is also the case that when much of a doctor's time is spent either in performing diagnostic and operative procedures or seeing to it that they get done, there may not be enough time left for studious pause and consideration of a patient's actual clinical needs.

In hospital settings of this kind, there are patients who may also become easy and unknowing victims of doctors with a certain special need. Such patients are not among those put through surgery just for financial gain, or those used as well informed subjects in approved experimental studies, but they come to be operated upon anyway because the resident doctors need to acquire surgical skills by "practicing" surgery under the supervision of staff physicians.

There are also those staff physicians who vie for academic prominence by working to advance what is called the "cutting edge" of medicine. New and sometimes unconventional procedures are performed, often upon unsuspecting patients.

It can happen, consequently, that the fundamental professional obligations of doctors to their patients are put aside in order to accommodate any number of these other priorities. In another context, inclinations of this kind would be labelled conflicts of interest. Although such violations of the patient-doctor relationship are not supposed to happen, and although once exposed they draw invariable institutional condemnation, there are no real foolproof safeguards in place affording patients the protection they need against these kinds of exploitation. In fact, it is impractical to implement a comprehensive, workable system for the protection of patients, medicine being as complex as it is, and the possibilities of surveillance being as limited as they are. As in all human ventures, be it as patients or in some other life role, we are forever at one another's mercy. Where we are generally unrealistic is to believe there is some kind of special immunity to, or protection from, the risks we expose ourselves to at the hands of doctors.

Rosana's vascular malformation was to become a surgical

obsession. Each millimeter of it had been visualized by multiple x-ray studies, from every angle, and in varied phases of its vascular filling, as injected dye substances were seen to course through its entangling, distended, arteries and veins. That did not suffice. Nor did any of the other tests which established its nature, size, and location, moderate a growing and consuming need to see it and to deal with it more directly, that is to have it in the flesh. Surgeons do seem to have that predisposition. To float radioisotopic particles through it, to see it by its magnetic resonance, or to know it by its Doppler measured blood flow, or by its radiographic computerized sectioning into CAT scan slices, was not to know it as surgeons are sometimes impelled to know such pathology. It needed to be had in real time and as a real life specimen. It needed to be had in the palm of a surgical hand. Unfortunately for Rosana, her care fell to doctors thus driven, and anxious also to enhance particular technical skills. They wanted to further a new method of excision. So intense was their preoccupation with what should have been nonapplicable issues of surgical technique, no attention was paid by them to the fact that this malformation was both too large and too strategically located for surgical excision to be a reasonable option under any clinical circumstance. The hospital record is also silent with regard to there having been any evidence, much less even a suspicion, of Rosana ever having had a hemorrhage. Rosana's endangerment was not from the possibility of rehemorrhage from her vascular malformation. She had never bled at all. It was from having fallen into the hands of aspiring and adventurous neurosurgeons.

There was a time when neurosurgeons attending national meetings were preoccupied solely with medical matters. Discussions and demonstrations would only concern issues of diagnosis, surgical technique, and decision-making regarding treatment. Nowadays, the display areas once devoted only to scientific exhibits have also become vast spaces in which dozens of instrument manufacturers hawk their wares. Doctors desert their lecture halls and seminars to go instead to these places. Here, sales representatives curry the favor of both institutional and individual buyers. Surgeons crowd around booths where the technical advantage of this or that instrument for a particular operative purpose is advocated. They are more preoccupied with *how* to do these operations, than *whether or not* to do them. Indications for surgery are commonly lost sight of. Videos are viewed showing the use of such devices during actual operations. The instruments often carry the name of the surgeon responsible for inventing them, he or she holding patent and royalty contracts with a manufacturer. In their turn, the manufacturers of these surgical instruments may have as much to say as the doctors about how certain operations are to be done. The instrument companies publish pamphlets for professional distribution, stipulating the manner in which each stage of an operation ought to be carried out, should it be performed with their product. For a considerable fee, they run seminars and hands-on workshops where operations are simulated with mannequins or tissue substitutes. Little of technique is left to individual judgement. And to do it "right" one must purchase their instruments. What are not delved into are the clinical justifications and the criteria for doing all of these operations. Nor the oft encountered complications.

One thing is sure. If a surgical instrument is manufactured, even if only for profit, it will come to be used anyway. Another dictum: certain operations would never be done but for the development of particular instruments. That includes operations which *should never* be done, irrespective of the availability of instruments making them feasible.

The viewing of such displays at medical conventions may remind an outsider of nothing so much as the automobile or other trade show last to occupy the same premises. It certainly does not project much of the idealizing, self-promoting puffery of medicine we are usually expected to ascribe credibility to. Nor does it augur very well for the clinical practice of appropriately performed surgery.

And when one enters one of the half empty auditoriums at one of these gatherings, it may not be to a medical presentation at all. The proceedings can very well be those of a medical lobbying effort, or of socio-economic action groups aligned with the American Medical Association in some kind of a joint bid for higher professional fees or other non scientific endeavors. Would doctors feel comfortable if these gatherings were open to the public and to their patients? And would hospitals want patients to know that they also have a hand in this? That they favor for staff appointments doctors having the skills to perform the widest variety of procedures made possible by so many different instruments? Such surgery swells their occupancy rate or makes use of their ambulatory surgical facilities. It cuts the overhead, pays for the expensive machines which generate other income, makes for big bills for services in both the operating rooms and laboratories. The result? Too much surgery and other kinds of care that can be unnecessary. What is to be expected from a system known to charge as much as two dollars for an aspirin tablet? Talk about the defense industry being inefficient or unscrupulous! At least the business of other business is just what we ordinarily expect from business. But the business of medicine, a supposedly higher calling, is all too often that of questionable medicine and transactions that are unduly money oriented.

So a tranquilized and drowsy young woman came to be rolled off to a surgical procedure feeling comfortably warmed by pre-operative sedation as well as by some vague inkling that before anything serious could possibly happen to her, before something in her head might "explode," she was to be saved. Alongside her stretcher walked the chief neurosurgical resident. To his mind, if this preliminary operation, one called an embolization, were to come off as scheduled, and be successful, he'd have an opportunity after that to perform his fourth operation for a vascular malformation of the brain. He was not thinking of the loveliness or the precious life of his patient. He was not turning over in his mind her medical needs or what might be an alternative to treating her in this surgical way. His thoughts were tactical and technical. They did not bear at all on what any of this might mean to her, but rather on what it meant to him. An engineer, fresh out of engineering school, would feel no differently on his way to a new construction site. This resident doctor was early out of school also. He was only four years graduated from medical school and looking to master the methods but not to shoulder the concerns one might think integral to the practice of neurosurgery, a bit different, one would ordinarily assume, from those of civil engineering. But when we do so, we can be awfully wrong.

This particular vascular malformation occupied a major portion of the left parietal lobe, a part of the brain concerned with sensation over the right side of the body, the kind of sensation relating to the perception of pain, touch, position sense or other kinds of critical awareness of the opposite limbs, as well as the shape, size, and textures of grasped or otherwise fingered objects. Because blood vessels of the malformation extended from the brain surface to a considerable depth, and were near fibers of the optic radiation concerned with vision, any attempt to excise them carried a high risk of damage to sight, as well as to sensation. Brain centers for speech function were also close by. In an effort to reduce these dangers, Rosana was to have an embolization procedure. The prospect of it helping her was no more than theoretical. This was not a method ever proven to be effective in the way it was to be used for her, and it was already reported to be associated with a high incidence of serious complications. The hoped for result was that if the blood stream could be utilized to carry small plastic pellets to the malformation, and that if they wound up lodged in its feeding arteries and obstructed them, the malformation would become smaller. Then, with its blood flow reduced, it was supposed to shrivel up. Presumably, as a smaller structure it would become easier to remove at a second stage of surgery to be carried out some time later. Rosana's alternative and quite real prospects for living a long and relatively asymptomatic life by doing nothing at all save for taking anti-convulsant medication, were to be traded off for a dubious speculation.

Embolization therapy has been used with only limited success to reduce the troublesome sound of a bruit, the swishing head noise a doctor could hear over her head, which can bother some patients but which she didn't hear at all. Embolization has also been tried in clinical circumstances wherein so much blood rushes into a malformation that the adjacent brain suffers a major and progressive reduction in its own blood flow. This latter difficulty, one she also did not suffer from, is called a "steal" syndrome and occurs in older individuals having their malformations for many years. The progressive neurological disability that it causes has occasionally been moderated or slowed by this kind of treatment. More often than not, however, the method doesn't work. And occasionally, the pellets have blocked arteries they were not intended to enter, producing paralysis or death. The difficulty is that once the pellets are injected into the carotid artery in a patient's neck, there is no way to direct or to arrest their passage as they float up into the blood vessels of the brain. The surgeon is just playing the odds. Chances are they will be swept into the most exaggerated or luxurious part of the circulation and that is the part which goes to the malformation, but there are no guarantees. The surgeon picks from a selection of little plastic beads hoping that the variety of their size will cause them to pile up beneficially and harmlessly where he would have them go. At best, this technique is uncertain if not arguable even when utilized for the control of such a "steal" syndrome. Any concept that it would improve the chances for a safe excisional removal of a vascular malformation at a later date was no more than a theory. It would be inappropriate, indeed, to even think in terms of what the criteria for that better result might have been in Rosana's case since the prospective operation, supposedly to be made less dangerous by this experimental prelude, should on no account have been considered. There was no indication for it and however well performed or safeguarded, it was destined to produce at least some serious neurological damage because of the dangerous location of the malformation in a vital brain area. Because Rosana's care had fallen to an attending neurosurgeon out to prove what could not be proven, she was ushered from her room by the neurosurgical resident and in about an hour the embolization procedure was begun.

It was carried out under local anaesthesia. There was no detectible change in her appearance on injection of the first few pellets. With the second injection, however, her face became suddenly suffused as she stiffened out, lost consciousness, and began to have convulsive movements of all four limbs. The left pupil enlarged. The right one followed. These were not like the seizures she had suffered before her hospitalization when she had stopped taking her medication. Now, they were the effect of sudden pressure upon the midbrain caused by a new and more deadly presence. This was "decerebrate rigidity." Quickly intubated by an anaesthesiologist and receiving intravenous mannitol, she was taken to x-ray for an emergency CAT scan. A large hemorrhage had suddenly occurred in the region of the vascular malformation. The malformation no longer slumbered as before. Secondarily, the brain had shifted from left to right to press against the midbrain and produce an uncal herniation.

Expeditiously, matter-of-factly, Rosana was now prepared for emergency operation. From the attending surgeon's demeanor there was little to be read of the disastrous nature of this unexpected turn of events. Driving his efficient calm was an insistent logic and the bravado rejection of anything to be gained by display of either dismay or fluster. There was to be no show of feelings for this Rosana, before or after her complication. These things do happen, and when they do, should they not be accommodated and dealt with straightforwardly? Besides which, well before this ruinous happening, the surgeon knew and had accepted full well that there could be problems with his novel technique. These were not well charted clinical waters. But was there still no capacity here for anyone to be stirred, to be shaken, by what portended from the sudden change in Rosana's condition? Was the doctor so driven to take part in a unique medical advance and to be credited for it that the personal bond and the obligations implicit in his unspoken but nevertheless real professional contract with this patient came to be traded off for a less empathic calling?

Upon her return from x-ray the stiffened body of the girl with alarmed, imploring pupils was unceremoniously yanked from the stretcher to an operating table where it yielded to the relaxations of anaesthesia. After the preliminary rituals of cleansing and draping, incision of the scalp was followed by the sounds of drill and saw as a plate of bone was reflected to expose the underlying dural membrane of the brain. Once this fibrous layer, appearing in this instance abnormally tense, blue, and bulging, is ordinarily divided, only a placid appearing brain should be exposed. But this was no ordinary circumstance. After release of the dura, no longer restrained, the vascular malformation was disgorged a full two inches beyond the opening in the skull. It flooded the operative field with an angry, pulsing torrent of bright red blood. There was little brain to be seen. The blood shot up in multiple geysers as high as a foot in the air, and before being covered over with cotton pads, managed to spurt across the gowns and face masks of the operating surgeons. Somewhere under the rapidly puddling blood and overlaid surgical pads, lay the tangle of vessels, exploding now and made this violent by the impudent provocation of the surgeon's attempt to embolize it. Even with three suction machines going, the flow of blood was so rapid that the operative field could not be cleared well enough for anything to be usefully seen. The neurosurgical resident could well despair of ever getting to try his beginner's hand on this particular malformation. And the attending neurosurgeon might well wonder how much, if included in a scientific paper, this case would unfavorably skew the optimistic data he'd hoped to report on his new method.

The plastic pellets had either not understood, or had mischievously refused to accept, their assigned destinations and purpose. The unpredictable had assumed its own control of the clinical situation. Instead of stopping close by their entry into the vascular malformation to occlude it and make it smaller, the pellets had slipped on through the larger arteries and lodged either in smaller ones or the draining veins. Blood was therefore not prevented from entering the tangle of arteries and veins, but rather from exiting. The consequence of its accumulation under pressure, and the limitation on it of a way out, was the bursting of several arteries with walls too thin to withstand this sudden extreme elevation of pressure. Those thin-walled dilated arteries of a vascular malformation are usually not exposed to even ordinary sustained levels of arterial pressure because capillaries, the smaller vessels usually intervening between arteries and veins, are absent in these lesions. The arteries, having now to empty their blood directly into large veins, are consequently not under much pressure because of this easy runoff. That is why the vascular malformations are called "shunts" and why they are said to constitute a "sink" for the flow of blood. They draw the blood and pass it much more rapidly from arteries to veins than is normally the case.

Blood poured from the multiple-holed arteries and over-flowed the operative field. For a desperate situation Rosana's doctors resorted to desperate measures. They incised her neck and placed a ligature around the carotid artery in hopes of reducing the pressure of blood flowing to that side of the brain and the malformation. It didn't work. There was no decrease in the rate of hemorrhage. The malformation, seemingly, was being fed too much of its blood from elsewhere. It was coming from two vertebral arteries and the opposite carotid, as well as the carotid artery of the same side and was not to be denied. Although blood was being transfused as quickly as possible by the anaesthesiologist, it was not feasible for him to keep up with the rate of its loss. Ever calm, the neurosurgeons, under-standing the futility of trying to arrest the vigorous flow of blood out of so many ruptured arteries, moved to limit the bleeding to one or just a few of them. With electrified wire loops and vigorous suction, they cut through the left side of the brain removing almost half of it, including in their excision the vascular malformation itself. Still, it refused to be deterred. From the depths of the hole so created, there issued a violent well-spring of hot, red, blood that there was no checking. The opera-tive field could not be controlled enough for the now consoli-dated bleeders to be identified. The pressure of pads, of pledgets, the surgeon's gloved finger tips, hemostatic agents, nothing... managed to materially slow down the hemorrhaging. Death came that quickly, violently, and insistently to confront their impotent composure. Its was the only real vitality in that oper-ating room.

Death stole the scene and lingered there, hovering over the lifeless body of the young woman. Its energy exceeded that of those who remained. From this scene, now so grimly charged, the attending surgeon exited. While others came to claim her body and to clean the soiled and bloodied room, littered with the debris of a lost, misguided cause, he dictated a five page commentary on the events attending her operation. As if the overstated length and extravagant detail of his account could attest to some sort of quality or dedication for the care he'd rendered.

One could say that Luis Rodriguez was more fortunate. He at least lives. His case was also different because his first convulsive seizure occurred at the age of fifty-eight. Except for geography, the dissimilarities then lessen. That his hospitalization was in San Francisco makes no particular point. It only affirms that malpractice knows no bounds. If the neurologist who saw him had prescribed dilantin and a repeat CAT scan in one year, his life would have continued much as before. It is even possible that with his seizures controlled by medication, he would have returned to truck driving. The neurologist had cared for many patients having convulsions and was capable of treating them. Never before, however, had he treated one with epileptic attacks brought on by a vascular malformation, or at least a malformation of which he was aware. Luis had such a finding in his CAT scan.

Years ago, before the advent of CAT scanning and other imaging techniques, patients with epilepsy were just given anticonvulsant medication unless something unusual was noted about their physical examination or their type of seizure. Now, all such patients have CAT scans, often revealing any number of brain abnormalities not previously encountered. Some of these abnormalities have to do with the epileptic symptomatology. Others do not. It then becomes a question of what to do about diseases being incidentally discovered that may or may not pose a problem for the patient in the future. Decisions also have to be made about the kinds of treatment required for symptom producing lesions, discovered now, because of these new techniques, at a much earlier stage of development than previously possible. Critical to such decision making is a reasonably comprehensive understanding of the natural course of many illnesses, including that of a vascular malformation, should one be discovered in this way.

The neurologist, never before having had to deal with a
vascular malformation, much less one probably causing epilepsy, turned elsewhere for advice. He would have been better
served by reading a textbook or a medical journal. It isn't that
he sought help from inappropriate quarters. He telephoned the
nearby office of the professor in a department of neurosurgery.
It will never be known how that doctor would have advised
him, had he actually been reached. He happened to be a professor who did not customarily answer phone calls for information. To telephone his office for that kind of assistance was
always to wind up with one of his resident doctors in training.
It was an integral part of his particular neurosurgical training
program. The residents, supposedly, were learning how to answer questions concerning their particular clinical discipline.
Unfortunately, this function was assigned them even before they
had learned very much about neurosurgery. Often, their inter-
rogators didn't come to learn what they needed to know, but
the professor managed to conserve time he deemed otherwise
valuable. A first strike against the patient because his neurologist was unacceptably ignorant about vascular malformations,
and another because Luis' care would now be controlled entirely by a neurosurgical resident who promptly accepted the
patient for transfer.

The wife was reassured to learn from the neurologist that
her husband would be "under the best man in town." She drew
additional comfort from the resident after Luis was actually
admitted to the hospital. She was to relax in the ease of being
told that the professor would see Luis every day and direct
every clinical move made in his behalf. The residents were "no
more than his agents," doing only what he instructed them to
do. Or so said the woman neurosurgical resident who had provided for Luis' transfer.

The professor, in fact, would have no knowledge even of
the existence of a man called Luis. The resident saw to it that
he was admitted, not as a private patient of the professor, but
to the "open" service, even though Luis was referred privately
and had insurance. Although the professor had ultimate responsibility for the way things were generally run in his de-

partment, the running of the open service was customarily delegated by him, under a rotating system, to assistant or associate attending neurosurgeons. It was these doctors who supervised all activities of the residents in training. In practice, their handling of things was rather a loose arrangement, permitting the residents a large measure of independent activity and discretion. The attending surgeons also had their private patients to care for as well as research activities leaving them only a limited number of hours for devotion to the "open" service and the instruction of the residents. It is no particularly guarded secret that this is how training programs are run nationwide. The attendings, nevertheless, were in the habit of claiming, particularly when things went awry in the operating room, that residents were supervised so closely, and in action they were together so much as one, that to distinguish what was done by their own more experienced surgical hands from the consequences of surgical manipulations by the residents, was impossible. They were a "team," every action of which was choreographed or controlled by strict regard for patient safety, as if to make the incredible insistence that a resident's surgical hands were but extensions of their own! If true it was a masterful feat of biological engineering! Ballet dancers and ice skaters would surely want to know the secret of their movements in perfect substitution and unison! Such boasts could certainly not be made by anyone really knowing anything about team play. Teammates do most things quite differently. Hardly then, could much candor be expected from the attendings who pretty much gave the residents free rein permitting them to operate much of the time without any supervision at all. There was little credence to be placed, either, in words out the mouth of this particular resident. What trust could there be for a doctor who knowing no more than the existence of a vascular malformation, would advise hospital admission for the "planning of surgery." A neurosurgical resident in her last year of training should certainly have known better. This one undoubtedly did. The temptation, however, to do one more operation of this kind before graduating, was for her, irresistible.

The needs of Luis and his family were to be secondary to

those of the resident who fancied that by the gain of such additional experience, she would be more capable of rendering
care to private patients when in a few months she would set up
her own practice.

If Luis were to live twenty more years and to attain the age
of seventy-eight, a life expectancy that would ordinarily be
projected for him, there would be at most, by the cumulative
rate of one percent per year, a twenty percent chance of his
malformation bleeding, assuming he had already bled once.
But he had never bled. The CAT scans showed no blood. His
spinal fluid was clear and colorless. Never in his life had he
complained of headaches. And the incidence of bleeding among
patients with an unruptured malformation is not even known.
Malformations are occasionally discovered at autopsy as trouble
free, asymptomatic, chance findings in patients dying of some
other cause at an advanced age.

Even if Luis had had an intracranial hemorrhage, the argument for an operation could not be persuasive for a man of his
age. Although there would then be a twenty percent chance of
recurrent bleeding over his next twenty years, no more than ten
percent of patients so affected will actually die from a hemorrhage. So through a projected age of seventy-eight there was
but a two percent chance of his death from a bleed. With surgical mortality for large malformations like his running at about
ten percent, only a fool or some terribly uninformed patient
would choose, in his circumstance, to be operated upon. As a
truck driver, he risked more every day on the streets of San
Francisco than he was threatened by his particular vascular
malformation, not to mention all the other potentially serious
and hidden conditions that may affect individuals his age.

There would be other reasons to avoid an operation. Surgical complications, including brain damage with neurological
disability, run even higher than ten percent among those who
survive operation. Furthermore, the malformation can easily
turn out to be only partially resectable, and incomplete removal
accomplishes nothing. As for the prevention of hemorrhage,
even excisions considered to be complete have been followed
by recurrent bleeding. Also, as commented upon in Rosana's

case, if the patient has seizures, they generally persist, irrespective of surgery being performed. It's fair to say that if Luis were this resident's father he'd not be having any operation.

Luis was not inclined to be inquisitive. "Don't bother the doctors," he told his wife. "They know what they're doing." Mrs. Rodriguez was not that trusting, especially after a few days acquaintance with this neurosurgical resident. Only once, did the resident, a very busy woman, take the time to enter into a discussion with her. Surgery would be carried out as soon as possible, and hopefully "before the time bomb exploded," but it would not take place until all of the necessary tests were completed. "What about the big man, the professor?" worried the wife. "When do we get to see him?" No direct response. Only the evasion that the professor, an even busier person than the resident, was supervising each and every aspect of Luis' care. At the right time, he would make an appearance, but there was really no point at all to his doing so until the "work-up" was completed. Then he would speak. She did not say to whom that prodigious communication might be made, or at what hour of the day or night, the professor might materialize in the patient's room. Luis' wife never did come to be comforted or privileged by such a meeting, and the resident had very few subsequent words for her. "That woman, always in such a rush to get away. You couldn't catch her even if you chased her down the hall! Such quick feet! Nothing but the work-up, the work-up, but how was it gonna be for my husband? Was it gonna be all right? That's all I ever wanted to know."

The purpose of a "work-up" is to evaluate the nature of the clinical problem so that appropriate treatment can be selected. This work-up was no more than a setting for a surgical performance already decided upon as soon as the vascular malformation was known to exist. And this neurosurgical resident was no marionette controlled by the professor. Unfortunately, he had no strings on her at all. Nor was she under anyone else's control.

Wherever you find hospitalized patients in large medical centers like this one, it can be much the same. Patients are there to be worked up, studied, discussed, scheduled, treated. Some are more "interesting" or "challenging" than others. They can be easy or difficult to treat; they may be looked after or neglected. Yet for all of the variation, patients themselves are as one in their overriding priority. They want doctors to care about them, and often they do not. So distracting is this need that patients casting about for caring doctors will scarcely notice the obvious ineptitude of a physician, or the physical inadequacies of hospitals they enter, as long as it is believed they are in the hands of people or institutions which are devoted to them as individuals. And once they decide there is reason to bestow their confidence, to their way of thinking, the very best that medicine or surgery has to offer will surely follow. Good treatment is thereby, supposedly, assured. But in reality they are but clinical passers-by identified only for the purpose of transit through an indifferent health care delivery process. And the providers of care, for the most part, have long ago abandoned any personally directed attitudes. Patients, by and large, are only a means to the particular ends of physicians and hospitals. Their treatment and their study are the way to reimbursement, intellectual stirring, excitement, reputation, self esteem, the business in short of the competitive state of being.

Rather than cast about for some medical Samaritan or what might be feigned as empathy in the medical arts, patients would be better served to seek after the best medical instrumentation and the most institutional resources. It is also important that they make their arrangements with an identifiable individual physician holding an established reputation for the treatment of their particular condition. If they choose, there are surveys that patients can turn to which give the operative track records for doctors and hospitals performing certain kinds of procedure. Things may still go wrong, but until medicine is more reliable, it is what patients should do.

The career of medicine, to some extent, has even purged caring from the ways of those more expected to hold it in trust. Women in medicine, all too often, have adopted the attitudes of their male colleagues. For patients still determined to find a doctor who will "care" about them, though they should primarily look for competence, they may do somewhat better with a woman physician. It is probably their best chance for an empathic professional relationship. The example of Luis, however, reminds us that even the instinct to nurture may not stand up very well under the acquisitive and aggressively self-serving demands of medical training and the need to "practice."

There are not many women in the field of neurosurgery, and those who aspire to that medical discipline do not find the going easy. They endure harassment, sexual and otherwise. They have a lot to prove to their professors, their attendings, the male residents, their own families often including physician members, and no less, to themselves. But their hardships and having to contend with discrimination hardly justifies what inclinations they have to beat the men at their own game or their own failures to concern themselves only with patients' needs.

Nothing could get in the way of this woman resident's operating upon Luis. She commandeered him. He was, also, her secret. Not only did she avoid his wife, she also steered clear of the professor. After all, for her there would be no further operating experience like this if the professor decided to take over this case. In only two weeks she was to graduate. Or suppose the professor were to decide that surgery was not necessary, was even contraindicated? She must have known enough, in spite of her oft-floated "time bomb" theory, to worry about her personal deprivation should anyone get wind of the real nature of Luis' illness. So to that end there was not even a mention of Luis' case in the weekly conference summarizing the stages of "work-up" for patients on the neurosurgical service. He was an unknown until the day before surgery was to be performed, at which time she sought out an attending neurosurgeon to supervise the operation.

"We've got a man on the service with an AVM. Would you be free on Tuesday?"

"Looks good to me. Do I need to see him?"

"Not really. Pretty straightforward. Why don't we just look at the films together?"

Just like that. Now there could be an operation. Then, no

more truck driving, a useless right arm and leg, problems seeing towards the right, and a severe impediment of speech.

The attending neurosurgeon was building his own reputation as an expert in the removal of vascular malformations of the brain. Working ordinarily with children, he rather welcomed this opportunity, offered him by the resident, to participate in an operation upon an adult. So keen was he to do so, he failed to reflect on the lesser tolerance of adults, compared to children, for brain removal or damage. Nor did he bother to consider that the necessarily higher long term risks of an unoperated malformation to the life of a child were much better justification for surgery than the very much lower short term risks to be incurred by a man who was fifty-eight years old. To him, the patient Luis had substance only as imaged by the x-rays. Luis was not a helpless man with anxieties and needs. He was a tangle of blood vessels in the left cerebral hemisphere of the brain, and a challenge to his skill in teaching how arteries can be dissected off the cortical surface in ways that avoid the brain damage which can result from removal of too much adjacent brain tissue. The patient, Luis, constituted no more than another opportunity for him to prove his surgical mettle.

That surgery upon those arteries might damage the brain, anyway, would just be a calculated, acceptable risk. And if, under his talented supervision, dissection by the resident proved not to be feasible, tempting her to suggest she try her hand at removing the malformation in toto, as part of an excised block of brain tissue, possibly to include part of the speech, motor, and sensory cortex, that was also a justifiable risk requiring bold assumption. Theirs were broad shoulders indeed. It never occurred to them, so focussed were they on what was "interesting or challenging," that if Luis were to be fully informed of the risks they were prepared to assume for him, he'd not be much inclined to leave his life in their hands.

Not once did the attending neurosurgeon ever see Luis in person during the entire course of his hospital stay. For him, Luis was no more than those x-rays and then a scalp shaved and prepared in the bright glare of the operating room for an incision intended to expose the skull and its contents. Never did he choose to ask when or if Luis had had a hemorrhage. Nor did he thumb through the medical chart to make his own assessment of the propriety of Luis' surgical candidacy as decided upon by the resident. Because he did not meet that responsibility Luis underwent an operation to prevent a second hemorrhage from a condition which had not caused him to have a first one.

As it turned out, the surgical technique employed by the resident was not too good. And the attending neurosurgeon was neither nimble nor quick enough to make up for it. The result was hemorrhage, and for it to be controlled, vital portions of the poor man's brain, along with the malformation, had to be excised or sucked away into tubings and drainage bottles. Other brain areas were surgically clipped or charred by electrocoagulation in an effort to arrest the bleeding. It is hard to understand of what value this unnecessary and crudely mutilative procedure could have been to the resident as an operating experience. And yet, word is she exulted in the completion of it and of "pulling him through." By some peculiar bent of mind, to do this kind of surgery was to prove her worth and to be made more qualified. She'd "been where Luis' soul was" and back. Hardly did it seem to concern her that for five days thereafter, his brain swollen, his left pupil dilated, Luis' life hung in the balance.

The occasional assertion, after serious consequences, that an operation was more difficult than anticipated, is surgery's belated way of claiming special dispensation for a kind of intrinsic, unavoidable, limitation. A surgeon is not likely to admit that on second thought, his operation was perhaps ill conceived, and that was the real cause for it to have turned out poorly. Or that someone else, but certainly not he or she, would have been more able to carry off the procedure satisfactorily. Rather, the bad result is couched in terms of it having constituted a sort of ambush of the surgeon by unpredictable or overwhelming disease, for which no surgeon could be expected to prove a match.

However, until the patient reemerges from the operating room in damaged form surgical capabilities are to be taken for

granted except for the customary advisement of serious complications being possible but unlikely, even when operations
are performed perfectly. Doctors aren't apt to confide that when
things go wrong it's generally because the doctor has made
sometimes one, but more often, a whole series of unacceptable
errors. Patients do not ever come to know this, so when the
patient or the relatives are confronted with the bad results of
surgery, they are usually inclined to accept newly itemized limitations and complications of surgery never known to them
before, rather than to suspect the inappropriateness of how either
diagnosis or treatment has been rendered.

Luis' wife did not see the resident again until the day after
surgery. She could surmise well before then that the operation
had been attended by unanticipated complications. And not
because the resident was nowhere to be found, or that a strange,
unfamiliar intern had been delegated to mumble something
about how well everything had gone until before the surgeons
could stop it, something "exploded" and that then there was a
technical "difficulty." People know instinctively that unless
things are clearly going very well, they are going badly. Luis'
apparent coma and his being on a respirator spoke more lu-
cidly than words for the result of his operation.

Almost in the same breath with the "difficulty" theme came
assurance that if he managed to improve just the least bit, Luis
would go to the best rehabilitation center in the world, and
conveniently, it was right there, just across town. Rarely is it
explained to patients or families that rehabilitation can never
bring back the function of missing or irreversibly damaged parts
of the brain. They are not told that all that can be accomplished
by such treatment is the learning of clumsy tricks by which, to
some degree, patients can cope by doing things awkwardly and
to a profoundly limited extent, but never in ways that are once
again natural or normal. Brain cells do not ever grow back. And
the ones that Luis needed in order to function properly were
now, along with the vascular malformation, resting in a jar of
formaldehyde in the neuropathology lab. Weeks later, when
microscopic slides of it would be projected on a screen for instruction of the residents, there would still be no question raised

as to how come this particular pathological specimen got to be removed, save for the fact of its having been discovered.

When neurosurgeons gather at national meetings much of what is said about patients and their treatment is apart from the format of scientific presentations. Doctors are equally influenced by what they hear at dinner, in corridors, over coffee, or in the bar. And what might Rosana's and Luis' doctors say in conversation about their own recent operating experience with vascular malformations? Like as not it would be heady stuff indeed! What a boon this or that instrument! How bloodless their surgical fields, and to what marvelous advantage the technique of embolization. Is it not fantastic that nowadays these things can be removed in spite of their size or location, with the patient spared any secondary neurological deficit at all! And then they might take leave of one another, buoyed by a sense of gain, of professional pride and ascendancy. Unmoved by lingering ghosts of patients injured, or even graveyards, there are doctors like these who seem to think they walk upon the water.

8

Michelle

STANDARD

*If it isn't feasible for a surgeon to operate at the optimal time,
every reasonable effort should be made to transfer that patient to
another qualified surgeon's care. The patient should be given a
full explanation for the importance of such an undertaking.*

W hen bleeding occurs from an intracranial aneurysm,
the purpose of operation is to prevent further hemorrhage. This kind of bleeding is different from that
brought on by a vascular malformation, in which instance hemorrhage is much less apt to recur or to be fatal. With aneurys-
mal rupture almost one third of the patients die before surgery
is feasible. Among those who manage to survive the first hemorrhage, further bleeding is associated with an even higher mortality. Most second hemorrhages take place during the first two
weeks of the illness. Because there is little disagreement about
statistics of this kind, it is hardly acceptable for a patient to
bleed a second time simply because a surgeon has not taken
advantage of his opportunity to intervene at a time optimal for
operation.

There are recognized situations when surgery does have to
be delayed. The brain can be too swollen for it to be safe. And
unconscious patients are not good candidates. There may be a
compromising degree of neurological disability. The patient may
be too old. The general state of health can be so tenuous as to
make surgery as dangerous or precarious as the risk of another
hemorrhage. There are other acceptable reasons to either post-
pone surgery or to not perform it at all. That a doctor wants

some time off or doesn't want another surgeon to operate in his stead are not ordinarily included among them.

Aneurysms are small, bubble-like dilatations of arteries at places of arterial branching which develop gradually because of a defect in the muscle layer of the vessel wall at that location. The aneurysm often balloons out until it thins to the point of rupture under the pressure of blood flowing through it. It is congenital in nature, that is predestined from birth because the defect in the muscular layer is something one is born with. The number of aneurysms which eventually rupture is uncertain. That's because aneurysms, like arteriovenous malformations, may also be asymptomatic findings discovered during the routine post- mortem examination of patients dying of other causes. When bleeding does take place, it is usually in adulthood. The symptoms may vary, depending upon whether blood is released primarily into the spinal fluid or destructively into brain tissue. Bleeding into the spinal fluid causes severe headache and stiffness of the neck by irritation of the meninges, the membranes covering the brain, and by elevation of intracranial pressure. If blood, leaking away from the aneurysm, should dissect through brain tissue, there are usually neurological deficits consistent with the functional loss of the particular brain areas damaged by that kind of penetration. There can be symptoms and signs of both types of involvement if bleeding takes place within the brain as well as into the cerebrospinal fluid.

Michelle is a thirty-nine-year-old woman who at the time of her first hemorrhage had bled only into the spinal fluid. Accordingly, she came under the care of a neurosurgeon because of severe headache. The second time she bled, it was into the brain. Although she was still hospitalized when that happened, her doctor was not there to treat her. He had gone off from Chicago to join colleagues at their national annual convention.

Bad luck? Nobody's fault? That it was quite another thing was the barely murmured contention of certain hospital staffers who were onlookers. One would have needed to be there to understand the situation as they did. Certainly, there is very little in the hospital chart that might draw the attention or occasion the suspicions of other doctors having for some routine reason to review it. That is especially true because the record was later altered with back-dated entries to suggest a continuity of professional attendance that never took place. Perhaps, if a doctor reading this chart just chanced to be an inquisitive neurosurgeon, he or she might wonder why, if the surgeon planned to operate upon his alert patient on the eighth hospital day, it could possibly be that surgery was never performed until the fourteenth day, which was two days after the patient became unconscious from a second intracranial hemorrhage. Curious or not, such a neurosurgeon, whatever his or her concern, would not be apt to raise such a question.

When her doctor departed, Michelle was entirely free of headache. She was no longer irritable or made uncomfortable by bright light. Those symptoms of meningeal irritation from the bleeding had subsided. The blood had been fairly well absorbed from the spinal fluid, and the inflammatory reaction of the meninges which enclose the cerebrospinal fluid in the "subarachnoid space" was on the wane. In that condition, she was a prime candidate for operation. Surgery would also carry very little risk for her kind of aneurysm. Attached as it was to a vessel known as the posterior communicating artery, it was a particularly easy one to reach surgically and there should have been no difficulty in placing a metallic surgical clip on it so as to exclude it from the arterial circulation. Michelle and her husband had agreed for the neurosurgeon to proceed and they were eager to have the operation over with.

The neurosurgeon came to her bedside on the sixth day. She was eating breakfast, looking rather well, pleased to have the bed rolled up so that at last she could be in the full sitting position and out of the partial recumbency which had only seemed to make her more prone to nausea and a dull pain near where her neck joined the base of the skull. Michelle was in a good mood, and so was her doctor. She, because of the final subsidence of very debilitating symptoms. He, now anticipating his scientific meeting and a leave-taking for it, everything being arranged for and approved as a university funded administrative absence. What less privileged individuals might call an all-expenses-paid junket.

Michelle was inclined to believe that her doctor carried a serious sense of dedication to her needs and that the responsibility he assumed for her welfare outweighed any other considerations. In fact, that would be why, although surgery had been originally planned for the following day, he now advised against it. It would not be proper for him to perform surgery and then, immediately afterward, set off for his convention. He preferred to operate upon his return when they could be certain of his being close by to attend her during the postoperative period.

Noble fellow! Far be it for him to fill her head with needless worry that the period of his absence would also be the precise time, when by all generally accepted statistics, the risk of a second hemorrhage was greatest! Why make her, not unnecessarily, but appropriately anxious? He would bear those concerns for her, and trust to luck for a favorable outcome of this added risk taking. It probably did not occur to him that Michelle had a right to know she was being placed in such jeopardy nor that if fully informed of the hazard inherent in delay she might prefer transfer to some other hospital and have the surgery done by an equally qualified neurosurgeon. Needless to say a surgeon like this one was not likely to get another surgeon on his own hospital staff to perform the operation. Cases of aneurysm surgery were not so easy to come by that he could afford to just give one away.

Not only was he noble, he was a stout young fellow as well, newly come to his own concept of how responsibilities and cares of this sort are to be borne and how not to worry patients unduly. Hardly would he be the one to appreciate that even when physicians do take a patient's state of mind to heart, they can't possibly feel the depth of concern patients themselves experience when they are permitted to make some choice, knowing full well that it may determine whether they live or die. And yet the inclination to deny patients such involvement is not uncommon among physicians, leading to a practice, as in this instance, of making decisions for patients that only patients themselves should be facing up to. This neurosurgeon wanted to perform Michelle's operation. He also wanted his time away. Under the circumstances, it was not right to arrange for both but it came down to that because he held his own wants to be more important than the medical needs of his patient.

Patients like Michelle often become not so much medical responsibilities, as gratifying cases by their numbers. Numbers that beyond being profitable, are also image making. In this second respect, they fall into various clinical categories for which, by the frequency of those numbers, surgical expertise can be claimed. One might, for example, encounter a neurosurgeon boasting of the completion of two hundred operations for just such a condition as Michelle's, an aneurysm of the posterior communicating artery. There is no way, of course, to know how well those operations were actually carried out. The inference of proficiency based upon the extent of clinical experience is commonplace, but only rarely tested. We have only started to do it now, finally, for coronary bypass and a few other kinds of operation. All the more reason for surgeons to covet aggrandizement based upon numbers alone. This bears an unseemly likeness to the collection of trophies by hunters. It is not far fetched to even suggest a kindred motivation of sorts for surgeon and hunter, a similarity between patient and prey. A surgeon of the kind caring for Michelle would also have nothing so much in common with a hunter as his immaturity. The juvenile attitude is, after all, characterized by a selfish and irresponsible nature. What possibly more selfish and irresponsible than a doctor abandoning a patient like Michelle in order to go off on a professional holiday?

Does it excuse him that he telephoned the neurosurgical resident every day regarding his patient? That he asked after Michelle? Was there new headache? Double vision? Stiffness of the neck? Was this circumstance extenuated by that seemingly solicitous inquiry? Or was it not also just more of the juvenile way of doing things? To know what is proper yet forbear, to feel guilt enough to have second thoughts, to wind up not responding accordingly but rather reaching out for constant reassurance that although he should never have abandoned her the patient was going to do well anyway, and no one would ever catch on... if that's not immature behavior, what is?

Such conduct was consistent with this doctor's usual kind of self-conscious role playing as a young, newly made chief of neurosurgery. Any observer with a sense of what was going on in his department could feel no more comfortable in his presence than, apparently, he with himself. Much of what he said or did induced that kind of embarrassment because of his quite premature assumption of responsibility for patients' lives, a role usually and better assumed by a more experienced doctor. What might naive medical students really conclude about a professional world in which the obviously immature likes of this doctor were put in charge of critical matters? What kind of role model had their university passed off on them? And to serve what sort of world? It would have to be the kind in which no one ages, where youngsters live on as youngsters, some to play awkwardly at being doctors. He could never be taken seriously as a chief of neurosurgery, and not because this is the age of immaturity, hardly anyone seeming right any more for leadership position. But because he had no capacity to be anything but self-centered.

With the second rupture of her aneurysm, Michelle's condition was far worse than it had been after the first hemorrhage. When it happened she was awakened from sleep by severe generalized head pains. These were bad enough to be described by her, months later, as a sensation that her head was bursting. Before she lost consciousness, she perspired profusely and experienced an intense nausea followed by retching and vomiting. There may also have been some double vision. A resident doctor, coming to examine her, found her blood pressure to be elevated. She was stuporous with dilated left pupil and weakness of the right arm and leg. The emergency CAT scan revealed that the new hemorrhage had torn into the brain itself and collected as a small clot in the deep part of her temporal lobe. Because the brain had not shifted very much in response to the clot, it could be assumed that although one pupil was dilated, it was from some cause other than the usually dreaded uncal herniation. The cranial nerve to the pupil, the oculomotor nerve, had probably been directly damaged by the bleeding.

Michelle was given cortisone in the hope of controlling some of the secondary brain swelling. In this instance mannitol could not be administered out of concern that there might be more bleeding if by giving it the brain should become slack and the tamponade effect of her swollen brain upon the bleeding site were to be eased too suddenly. After five days of fluctuating levels of consciousness, she started to improve. By then her doctor was back in town. Up until then he'd supervised her care by telephone.

Now he determined to be deliberate, to act, and thereby to introduce still another kind of risk. There would be no further delays about her surgery. He operated on the day of his return. The clot was removed and the aneurysm was isolated from the vessel upon which it was located by the application of a surgical clip. No further bleeding could occur. There could also be no further function of those parts of the brain now damaged by both the second hemorrhage and the surgery.

Most neurosurgeons would not have operated at this time. Michelle had not regained full consciousness. There was still a significant degree of brain swelling. Patients, as a rule, do better if allowed to improve before surgery is performed in instances of acute brain hemorrhage, unless an operation must be attempted for removal of a life threatening clot, producing the signs of uncal herniation. Whereas previously he had failed to operate upon Michelle when her condition was optimal, now he rushed her to surgery in a weakened condition. The young chief was born, it seemed, to be wrong, and all too many of his patients, to misfortune.

Clinical judgment, surgical in particular, is acquired in large part through experience. That is not to say that young surgeons cannot possess it. Indeed they may, if they operate often enough, read extensively, and if they are receptive to the teachings of other neurosurgeons who have seen more patients than they have over a longer stretch of time. Senior surgeons may also have better, more extensive, command of the medical literature. But this young chief was not the sort of doctor who would ask any other member of his department for their opinion or advice about anything. He knew it all. Hard to imagine, though, where he might have come by his oft proclaimed experience with "the hundreds" of cases he so frequently referred to, not being much more than two years out of training. And hard also for him to learn from other neurosurgeons, when his habit was to interrupt anything they might volunteer with interminable commentaries of his own.

The young chief's hasty operation upon Michelle, however, had nothing to do with surgical judgment. What her condition might be following an operation that was performed too soon and at a time she could ill tolerate it, was not likely to have influenced him. What had to be prevented, quickly and at any cost, was death by still a third hemorrhage, or by the effects of this second bleed, at a time when no operation had yet been performed. After all, she had been a clear candidate for operation shortly following admission to the hospital. And then there came that unaccountable, unduly long lapse of time when she just lay there with nothing being done for her. Even this oddly overindulged young neurosurgeon could not chance the notoriety of that kind of exposure. So, late or not, Michelle had to become a documented, operated patient. And if she should succumb to the effects of such ill advised, poorly timed, precipitous surgery? Well, everybody knows that brain operations are a serious business, and that patients commonly die of them. At least he'd have that cover. There is also the unfortunate prevailing assumption that the performance of a major operation means that all other treatment options have been exhausted. The patient is considered to have had everything done that was possible. Prevailing medical attitudes, however, may not on simple applied logic or circumspection prove out as unassailable wisdom. The devil, as always, is in the details, and they hardly ever surface or are uncovered. As for some later recitation of circumstances associated with a complication such as this one, or even with a death on this young doctor's neurosurgical service, there was not apt to be any kind of conference in which it might be conceived or speculated that treatment should have been rendered differently, much less that serious consequences could have been avoided.

Michelle lives, but she is handicapped. Her eyes do not scan properly and she will always experience double vision. There is weakness of her right side. Hard to say just what else is wrong to make her husband so insistent she is nowhere near being the same woman as before. That's his way of complaining about a difference in her personality, that fragile ingredient binding people together. Although she has survived, his essential wife has left him, simply because her doctor skipped town.

Opportunities for the husband to complain were extremely limited. The young chief follows his postoperative patients only briefly. Once three months have passed they are sent back to their referring doctors. Office hours are for new cases. They cannot be taken over by those already having had surgery. The aftercare of postoperative patients must be handled elsewhere. The office is used almost exclusively to search for new candidates for operation. It is of no consequence to the young chief that family doctors and other referring physicians may be poorly equipped to handle the problems of postoperative neurosurgical patients. Those needs of his patients must yield to his well organized schedule.

What Michelle's husband could somehow manage to convey by way of concerns about his wife was not responded to with either consolation or practical advice. Rather, he was told how much he and his wife "needed to appreciate" just how lucky they had been. The young chief had come back in the very "nick of time"! Were he to have delayed his return for even a few hours, "Michelle would not have made it." Fortunate indeed were they that finally he'd had his fill of the convention, that there were no more papers to be heard, dinners to be attended, exhibition booths to be visited, important association officials to be gladhanded.

The essential trick is to get patients like Michelle out of the hospital. If only they make it through the exit doors, that particular medical or surgical venture is an unqualified success. The person leaving may be an entirely different kind of individual from the one who entered. Personality, intellect, mood, physical capability, all of that, may have deteriorated. There is no inclination to score such things. Patients with irreversibly damaged neurological functions are often noted in the "progress" sheets of hospital charts as showing "no essential change" until headed for home or to rehabilitation centers to complete their so called "recoveries." Should they remain in the hospital such patients become a liability because their beds are sorely needed to accommodate new high-ticket candidates for profitable procedures and operations. There's not much money to be made from the day-to-day needs of those who might tarry only because their care has not met ordinarily held expectations. These days, no insurance company, past a certain point, will pay for such hospitalization. Departed promptly, however, patients become an asset. Then money can begin to flow back to doctors and hospitals for new services rendered to new patients.

Also, once gone, patients are ticked off as a different kind of credit. By their previous presence they have automatically earned the medical institution a kind of tribute, something like interest on an account compounded by deposit and the passage of time. For having completed this or that sort of treatment, or this or that operation, under some specific diagnosis, in whatever manner, regardless of the result, a claim can be made of such clinical activity as a measure of institutional and specialty expertise. That is how hospitals stay accredited and how residency training programs maintain their approval ratings.

Of course, patients of any kind, once gone, can be welcomed back. Their return, under some circumstances, may even be encouraged. Opportunities to reoperate, if considered "necessary," provide another valuable advantage. For example, a patient with an incurable, slowly growing brain tumor, upon reoperation may constitute an important hospital and specialty service statistical credit, as well as a significant asset, generating more money. There are, in fact, training programs that are only marginally qualified. Their approval is no more than conditional because they do not offer doctors in training sufficient opportunity to perform surgery or to examine patients. It has been known to happen that such a training program may only "stay alive" by routinely scanning its lists for the purpose of running certain patients back through the diagnostic and operative mill. If that patient with the incurable slow growing brain tumor should then be advised of possible benefits from having just a little more tumor removed, or some pressure relieved, who, desperate and unsuspecting as such patients usually are, would they be to argue with their doctor?

Even if Michelle had left the hospital, not incapacitated, but in full command of all of her faculties, both she and her husband would still have departed unaware of the lapses in her care. Most medical facilities cultivate and count upon a tightlipped atmosphere. But considering her mental state and the especially emphatic insistences of her neurosurgeon, it can be safely said that she and her husband were especially ignorant of what had happened to her. The system and her doctor had worked hand in hand.

9

Eliani

STANDARD

The care of critically ill patients should be expedited and directly supervised by a single, properly licensed physician, fully qualified to treat that condition. Divided responsibilities are not conducive to satisfactory patient care. In such circumstances medical students and first level residents must restrict their learning experiences to observation of the care rendered by those more knowledgeable and experienced. They should strictly avoid any "hands on" compromise of time crucial to the patient's best interests.

The six-month-old infant had been no trouble for her seventeen-year-old single mother until the night she started to vomit and to cough. At the emergency room her temperature was 105°. The doctor did not agree with the mother's observation that the baby's neck seemed to arch. He insisted that she was "dead" wrong.

Stiffness of the neck, especially that which leads to arching, is medically designated as the condition of nuchal rigidity. It is also the diagnostic indicator of meningitis, an infection of the spinal fluid pathway. Nuchal rigidity is a very reliable and easily elicited physical finding. The young mother knew nothing about that. All she was wondering was why the baby had suddenly started to arch her neck. The young doctor remembered much of what his books had said about meningitis, but it availed him not at all, because he had never acquired the proper knack for testing so ordinary a thing as stiffness of the neck. Also, he didn't have enough common sense to appreciate that when a mother says the infant with whom she spends all of her time looks "very different" to her, those are comments which should command his serious attention. He can very well take them to the bank!

At 1:00 A.M. the mother returned home from the emergency room with her Eliani. It was snowing. The bus trip had required a transfer and taken a good hour. Unlikely that even this cold journey reduced the infant's fever any. And there was no other possibility of that happening because she'd received no medication for the baby's elevated temperature. Besides which, the mother had no thermometer, nor had it been suggested that she get one. It is not known, therefore, what the baby's body temperature may have been over the next twenty-four hours. There's not much to be learned from the emergency room record, either. No blood count was done. If someone did take the time to palpate the infant's head for bulging of the forward part between the frontal bones, the fontanelle, a sign of elevated intracranial pressure, the results of that examination were never entered. The record did include the diagnosis of an upper respiratory infection and the suggestion of reevaluation in the pediatric clinic after two days. "Not to worry. Just bring her back in two days." Nose drops, cough medicine, and an antihistamine. Routine pediatric medicine by the book, a handbook carried in the doctor's pocket. Some book! Some doctor!

The next trip to the hospital, about twenty-four hours later, required an ambulance. By then, the baby was having continuous generalized seizures. So if the neck did remain stiff, in the presence of all those convulsions, that important finding would be hard now to verify. The entire body of the infant was going into frequent spasms and she appeared to be somewhat blue about the lips. Her pulse was three hundred. Blood pressure was low, and the infant, because of continuous vomiting and persistent fever, was severely dehydrated. Intravenous fluids were started and a neurology attending was called for advice but only regarding medication to stop the seizures. Phenobarbital was given on the neurologist's recommendation; however, she did not actually come to the hospital to examine Eliani until two days later. Nevertheless, that first neurological consultation, conducted solely by telephone, came to be dutifully entered into the record by one of the pediatric residents.

This is not supposed to happen. Even if doctors call in a prescription to a pharmacist for some patient well known to them, it is hazardous to practice medicine that way for any new condition. But to call in medication for a critically ill hospitalized infant, admitted as an emergency, never seen before that same day, and never personally examined, was to lack proper regard for that baby's life.

If there exists enough clinical concern for emergency consultation to be necessary, then it needs to be a real one that includes review of the hospital record, independent history taking, and a thorough physical examination. Good doctors do not prescribe treatment by telephone based upon another physician's history and examination, particularly for patients that are dangerously ill and who have been seen only by medical beginners. Poor people, unable to pay for consultations, are typically dealt with in this negligent way. Affluent patients are only rarely subjected to third rate consultations carried out between doctors by telephone, in hospital corridors, or in stairwells, although it can happen to them also, according to your average daily newspaper.

These young pediatric residents needed better supervision in matters other than control of this infant's seizures. If meningitis is to be treated properly, time is of the essence, and yet Eliani did not have a spinal tap so that the spinal fluid could be examined microscopically or cultured until more than two hours after hospitalization. And although the ordinarily clear spinal fluid was loaded enough with inflammatory cells for it to be very cloudy when merely eyeballed, antibiotic medication was withheld for several hours. Meanwhile, time was being further wasted by the taking of skull x-rays and the performance of tests having no relevance at all to the quite obvious condition of bacterial meningitis.

Finally under antibiotic treatment, the baby continued, nevertheless, to convulse. The appearance of an infant having sustained generalized seizures rarely fails to evoke alarm among even seasoned clinical observers. Limbs jerk back and forth in

a set rhythm of movement, or extend rigidly as if straining to
assume the quadrupedal posture of another time. The thrashing and the contorting are demonic, deaf to any insistence or
entreaty to stop, immune to any prayer that the arms and legs
go gratifyingly limp. Better almost for them to go lifeless (that
horrible thought could cross an impatient mind) than that they
continue to perform this dreadful, seemingly agonal, burlesque
of purposeful movement.

There could be no stopping the convulsions as long as the
treatment being given was as inappropriate as it turned out to
be. And they would be the cause of an otherwise entirely preventable degree of brain damage had treatment been different.

Patients do not breathe properly during generalized convulsions. There are sustained contractions of the respiratory
muscles, taking place because of the seizures, which interrupt
the chest wall movements responsible for drawing air in and
out of the lung. Respirations are impaired to the extent that
oxygen is not taken in properly and carbon dioxide builds up
in the blood stream. But under conditions of brain infection and
high fever the brain requires even more than the normal amount
of oxygen, not only for brain cells to be able to function, but so
that they are not permanently damaged. As in the case of brain
swelling or hemorrhage due to injuries, here also, the retention
of carbon dioxide causes an increase in intracranial pressure by
virtue of the action of carbon dioxide to dilate the cerebral arteries. Intracranial pressure goes up and blood flow to the brain
may become progressively diminished. Each unfortunate change
instigates others, all part of a cycling series of setbacks and
stresses, with the brain suffering more and more as time passes.
By virtue of the seizures, much of the brain is discharging its
cells chemically and electrically, bringing about unusual demands for the oxygen and glucose needed to sustain cellular
energy and integrity. It is, indeed, the worst possible time for
that to happen, a time when oxygen is in short supply and
intracranial pressure is on the rise. The brain cells begin, therefore, to die.

It was critical to stop the seizures and also to lower the
infant's body temperature. The fever tended to increase even

further the brain's already high oxygen requrement, a requirement that was not being met. In cases of meningitis the fever
usually responds to the administration of appropriate antibiotics and various cooling measures. That much the doctors did
finally accomplish. What they completely overlooked for two
days, however, was an unmistakable indication that the convulsions, rather than being related to the fever or to the infection,
were the result of very low levels of blood serum calcium. They
were simply not heeding the laboratory reports, reports being
faithfully attached to the hospital chart and posted in the baby's
record. So instead of giving the infant intravenous calcium,
which would have stopped the convulsions quickly, they gave
increasing amounts of the drug phenobarbital which had been
recommended by the neurologist, the one whose habit it was to
give advice by telephone. Phenobarbital is an excellent and time-
honored anticonvulsant drug, but not for this kind of seizure
state. As soon as this oversight was finally recognized and calcium gluconate given, the seizures were brought under control.
That, unfortunately, was not before the infant had received many
overdoses of phenobarbital and was allowed to persist in the
convulsive state for an unduly long period of time. It was then,
at last, that the pediatric junior residents realized their need for
a real, live, neurological consultant to actually come to the
infant's bedside. They summoned, once more, someone in that
medical specialty to examine the baby. This time a neurology
resident responded. It was she who pointed out the reports of
low serum calcium which had been ignored.

Why order so many blood tests day after day and make all
of that bruising penetration of an infant's fragile, elusive, veins,
if when the results are abnormal they will be overlooked, or
even worse, be noted and recorded but still not lead to correc-
tive treatment? "Mistakes" of this kind have occasioned "human factor analyses" to come upon the medical scene by the
encouragement and insistence of no lesser organizations than
the American Medical Association and the Joint Commission
on Accreditation of Hospitals. To the fore now, in the approach
to medical negligence, comes the study of the reasons for human error. They are supposed to be no different than what

occasions planes to fall from the sky and trains to pile up on one another. But is this no more, really, than a smoke screen, a subterfuge, allowing all the other kinds of medical negligence to go unresponded to and to permit doctors such as these to hide behind the insistence that after all is said and done, to err is but a human thing? And so no fault, let us merely concentrate upon coming up with what fail-safe measures we can devise to at least limit such occurrences. I cannot speak to concerns for safety in either the aviation or the railroad industry, but I suspect that the issues there are a good deal simpler and different than in the practice of medicine. And I know for certain that nowhere in the case of Eliani or in any of the other examples of medical negligence I am citing does a single one of these casualties of medical practice come down to the problem of innocent, excusable, human error. About being human, yes. It is, rather, about being unable as a human to measure up to one's subscribed to obligations. And the human toll for this is enormous.

Those affected by the most serious kinds of neurological negligence are least likely to seek redress on their own. That task falls to their relatives. Only those just slightly or moderately injured can personally seek such satisfaction. And of those most victimized, few are actually known. How could they be? Who might have the special knowledge needed for awareness of the often grievous manner of their passing or hurt? Many of the worst cases are not even suspected. And when they are, and the issue is joined, are the victims or society truly served by the controlled, so-called impartiality of any of our peer review or judicial processes? Modern society eschews retribution in kind. And by negligence of the sort involving the baby Eliani, injury was certainly not intended. But if the day to day operating conduct of the physicians responsible for her ultimate damage was their deliberately chosen and institutionally endorsed routine, and if it was a poor enough one for them to expect bad results from it sooner or later, should there not be some special way to signify how wrong that was? Some punitive action or penalty that might at least deter such irresponsible medical behavior?

The attending physicians responsible for running this pediatric department gave each one of their doctors in training, the residents, an opportunity to learn by practicing medicine on this unfortunate baby. At a time when the outlook for variable ranges of recovery versus the possibility of death itself, hung on the appropriateness and the timing of treatment, medical amateurs were permitted to waste those important hours and overlook both diagnostic signs and pertinent, critical, laboratory data. What was to happen to Eliani as a victim of this flawed medical methodology must have already happened in that hospital on other occasions. It would have had to. Patients could not possibly escape being regularly injured by such a slipshod system.

No fully qualified attending pediatrician was on hand to supervise the activities of the medical students, interns and residents, assigned to patient care. Those relatively inexperienced doctors, commensurate with their level of training, were actually supervising one another! Intern, assistant resident, junior resident, senior resident, each in his or her turn wrote a history, performed an examination, made a differential diagnosis, and proposed a treatment plan for Eliani, the final issuance and implementation of orders being authorized by the chief pediatric resident. Infants with some other condition might tolerate such trifling away of their time, but not one with bacterial meningitis. Even an inept third year medical student was given some minutes to work on this poor baby. He listened to her chest, palpated the abdomen, looked in all of the various body orifices, and wasted some of the precious dwindling moments of an infant about to die, practicing things better reserved for the well baby clinic. And when the laboratory data was reported back to the hospital chart, it was examined by young doctors who only caught those obvious abnormalities associated with infection, but not the unanticipated finding of a depressed serum calcium. It is incredible that these medical novices did not do better on at least that score! It did not require an experienced pediatrician to observe the variance of calcium from normal. Lab reports always indicate alongside any reported value what is the acceptable range of normal ones.

They even flag or highlight those that are abnormal so that they may be quickly noted by the doctor. But when doctors who are beginners learn by working under their own supervision, they get neither proper instruction nor the example of a reliable discipline of diligence or thoroughness. They are exposed to no beneficial role model, and they are not held to any high standard of conduct. They structure their own concept of what they should be like and of how they should practice medicine.

By and large, patients are more often treated this way when they are hospitalized as uninsured admissions at teaching institutions or when they have no doctor of their own. Although the name of an attending doctor must be entered in the hospital record as the physician assuming responsibility for each patient's care, commonly this is no more than a formality made necessary for meeting the legal requirements of institutional and residency accreditation, and to assure that the hospital will eventually be reimbursed for its services. Hospitals are not eligible to receive money for care that's actually rendered by interns or residents. They are considered to be mere learners by insurance carriers and funding agencies. So eventually, attending doctors must at least initial the chart in each and every important place the young doctors have placed their own signatures. But they hardly pay much attention to what is being countersigned or vouched for. When the record room summons them, attending physicians countersign charts by the dozens, months after patients have been discharged, often not remembering them or ever having known much about them. There can be countersigned charts for patients not ever seen by an attending physician. But just before inspections by the hospital accreditation commission, doctors are notified. The word goes out and the record room becomes a very busy place indeed. Hardly room enough, at times, for doctors to crowd in and sign away at the stacks of records.

Except for making occasional rounds or being available for advice, attending physicians like these are infrequently present on the medical wards. They are more likely to be with their private patients. This entire enterprise is a deliberate fraud and certain to fail the needs of all kinds of sick people, people who are usually unaware of how they are being used, practiced upon, and cheated of the treatment to which they are entitled and for which all of us have paid. Can there ever be sufficient amends for causing patients to be crippled or to lose their lives under such a system? How does this kind of mayhem get to be called nothing worse than the "malpractice" of medicine? Even when seriously ill, financially disadvantaged supplicants for medical attention at large private teaching hospitals are usually first seen by physicians with minimal experience. The treatment of these patients is geared to the provision of a learning experience for medical students and doctors in training. In municipal or state run hospitals affiliated with universities, it is the same. Here, local and federal tax revenues pay for that kind of care. It should be remembered that for private hospitals as well, public funds are allocated to serve the health needs of the indigent, but are expended in the same irresponsible way. Largely ignorant of, or indifferent to how the less fortunate are treated, we continue to spend tax money to defray the cost of a kind of medical care that is dispensed without conscience, that cannot be justified.

Imagine, for a moment, how it would be to know you are dangerously ill, but that the doctor assigned to you, by virtue of inexperience, is incompetent. And to know that this physician is not there by the mere bad luck of your particular draw, but as part of a plan approved at the highest levels of academic medicine, as well as national and local public health policy. So much for the unrealistically assumed expectation of a solicitous or humanistic attitude on the part of either organized medicine or public health planners! They have deemed it acceptable for a patient in his or her death throes to be pondered over by medical students, fumbling unlicensed interns or residents, as well as other physicians not long out of medical school, rather than to insist that every patient must be treated effectively, directly, and expeditiously by someone who knows what he or she is doing. Imagine further being evaluated by a doctor knowing no more than what may be recalled from a lecture or a textbook, or from a similar case possibly encountered on teaching rounds. Consider that foreign medical graduates working as interns or residents have the added handicap of problems with language. Suppose that for lack of there being any certainty as to the specific tests required, having more performed on you than necessary, or undergoing the wrong ones, and then, finally, being assigned a doctor with marginal ability to interpret or to comprehend the results.

All of this was easily foreseen, but was advocated and implemented anyway on a national level on the premise and the promise that such young doctors would never be turned loose without close, tight, supervision by qualified attending physicians. The premise was wrong, the promise never kept. How to estimate the number of lives abbreviated or compromised by such universally unfulfilled and ignored assurances?

And if on one of those infrequent occasions that some jury decides that compensation is to be made, or blame placed for such an institutional failure, who is to be ultimately charged with that burden? Whatever the jury's word in the matter, like as not the invariable appeal to a higher court will be floated. After all, the defendants will ask once more, as they usually do at trials stemming from such incidents, is a hospital any more than mortar? Or is it plausible to contend that anyone on the institutional governing board could actually know a specific circumstance, or intend injury to a particular patient? How can it possibly be alleged that the chairperson of a clinical department is a guilty agent when the name of that aloof and remote individual appears nowhere in the hospital record? Don't the well respected and recognized organizations established for the purpose of medical and surgical certification of hospitals insist upon close supervision, and "aren't we approved by them"? How can "our young doctors," not even licensed to practice, for whom others are responsible, be held to any account? And the attending doctors? What, conceivably, could they have done for the patient, if no one called them when they were needed? Why were they even named in the suit, in the first place? So many questions! So many defense positions! So many medical miscreants! Rather than wait years for a final resolution of such claims by the grindingly slow judicial process, settlements providing for the reduction of jury awards and the dropping of charges against numerous defendants are often agreed to. Some money is paid out but only under the stipulated understanding that all of the discussions and agreements are to be held in strict confidence under penalty of the law. The court records are sealed and the settlement of the suit carries no implication of anyone actually being at fault. The money to be disbursed is as small as can be arranged for. Only if it exceeds a certain amount will a doctor's name be forwarded to a national registry. Even then, no details of what has transpired are submitted. Whatever money is paid out, it repairs no damage, brings back no life. And nothing has happened to provide incentive for changing the system. Everything, except the patients and their families, goes on as before. Little Eliani's case would turn out no differently.

Thirty-six hours after hospital admission the report of a low serum calcium was brought to everyone's attention by the neurology resident. As soon as calcium gluconate was given intravenously, the seizures began to subside. No one, however, paid any attention to the fact that the phenobarbital, although no longer needed to stop the seizures, continued to be administered and in a very high dosage. Gradually, under the cumulative, sedative effect of that drug, the baby became more and more lethargic.

This hospital chart was enormous. Everyone had something to say. Each day the medical students and all of the residents filled pages with their varied observations and speculations. Among the notations were confessions of uncertainty regarding the appearance of the infant's optic discs when her eyes were examined with an instrument called an ophthalmoscope. Some said "questionable papilledema." Others said "normal," or "hyperemia," or "blurring" of the disc margins. Appearances beyond normal of the kind mentioned are all indications of increased intracranial pressure. No one thought to ask an attending physician to resolve this critical question. These were just interesting findings for these young doctors to record laboriously in the record. They also had differing opinions regarding the anterior fontanelle of the skull, that space on the forehead which infant's have between the frontal and parietal bones and which may be palpated for tension. Some could not feel it at all. Others found it to be flat and no more than finger tip in size. One doctor thought it full, even tense. All quite fascinating to some, or mundane to others, but not a basis for any of them, of the legitimate concern findings of this sort should provoke under fluctuating conditions of mounting intracranial pressure. An elevated pressure was in fact beginning to threaten this infant, and some of those described appearances of the fontanelle were signs ordinarily alarming to physicians who know their medicine, but that was not the case for these doctors.

And then, there were the pupils. They varied in size and in reaction to light. Sometimes the left one was dilated. On other occasions it was the right. Only the requirement to record such variation was met. The obligation to place a reasonable interpretation upon it, and the necessity for considering its relationship to the possible swelling of the optic discs or the occasional bulging of the fontanelle, were never considered at all. Due to infection, seizures, oversedation, and impaired respiration, the brain was now swelling to the point of pushing an uncus, sometimes the left one, at other times the right, against the midbrain. There was still an equilibrium, a balance of sorts. An actual herniation of either uncus had not yet occurred. At this point further diagnosis and treatment could have been effective in preventing it. The baby got no such treatment. Instead, another spinal tap was performed.

At the time it was carried out, not only was a spinal tap unnecessary, it was too dangerous to be considered. If there is any clinical or x-ray evidence that the brain is swelling and intracranial pressure mounting, especially if that swelling is greater on one side of the brain than the other, spinal taps are usually avoided. By the optic disc, the pupillary, and the fontanelle changes, the doctors had at least three indications of such swelling and in spite of those warnings they proceeded to tap the infant anyway. The danger inherent in such a procedure is that it may bring on an uncal or other kind of herniation. As spinal fluid is removed in the region of the lower back, and as it also leaks afterward through the punctured spinal membrane, the dura, into the tissue spaces of the spinal canal, the brain is caused to shift from locations of high pressure and limited room toward areas in which space and lower pressure have been provided by the removal of spinal fluid. The first parts to shift may be either the uncal portions of the temporal lobe or the cerebellar tonsils at the base of the brain. Because the left cerebral hemisphere of the baby was more swollen than other areas, it was the left uncus that was the more likely to herniate. If on the basis of all of the suspicious signs available to them, that spinal tap had been avoided, a CAT scan performed, and treatment to reduce the intracranial pressure instituted, this baby should have done much better. It could have been spared the uncal herniation which now occurred.

It is difficult to understand the rationale for performing the spinal tap. By now, the bacterial organism causing the meningitis had been identified and the infant was under treatment with appropriate antibiotics. The signs of meningitis were clearing. The fever was down. The neck was no longer stiff. The primary remaining clinical problems were the sedative effects of overdosage by phenobarbital and the fluctuating intracranial pressure. They were the ones needing to be addressed. As it turned out, study of this second specimen of spinal fluid revealed nothing more than the favorable trend that should have been recognized and anticipated by the clinical signs of improvement. There were many fewer inflammatory cells. The spinal fluid sugar was back up to normal and the previously elevated spinal fluid protein level was down. To avail the hospital record of that kind of data, and to satisfy the misguided curiosity of the doctors who performed the tap, the infant was now to be jeopardized by an overburdening series of successive injuries stemming solely from that badly chosen procedure.

The morning after the spinal tap the infant was found to be spastic and less responsive. The left pupil was dilated and non-reactive to light. A pediatric resident who charted these findings ordered an immediate CAT scan of the head and re-evaluation by neurology. Until then, the only neurological consultation, other than the one by telephone on the day of admission, had been that conducted by a first year resident in neurol-

ogy regarding the low serum calcium. She, like the other train-
ees, had not picked up on the obvious overdosage with phenobarbital. She had failed to warn against another spinal tap or
that should one be carried out the infant would require very
careful observation for a possible uncal herniation, having, like
the others, not appreciated what was happening to the intracranial pressure.

Now, summoned back to the infant's bedside, because what
should have been foreseen and avoided, had in fact transpired,
she did not know what needed to be done other than to bolt
from the ward and search for her own attending. It escaped her
notice that the CAT scan ordered six hours earlier because of
the dilated pupil had not yet been carried out. It did not occur
to her, either, that it might be a good idea, because of the enlarged pupil, to start the customary treatment with mannitol or
to summon a neurosurgeon.

In another few hours she was back with an attending neurologist. This new doctor had all the right kinds of reflex reactions and suggestions. "STAT CAT scan. STAT Mannitol. STAT
neurosurgical consultation. STOP phenobarbital." But because
she was not accustomed to the bother and the nicety of seeing
to it that her recommendations in her note of procedures needing to be done "STAT" were subsequently written as order and
implemented as an emergency, nothing happened. To the minds
of some doctors, doctors like her, the essential responsibility is
to enter the required consultative opinion into the record. Other
doctors, at their discretion, can accept it or not accept it and
come to their own conclusions about acting on it, but the
consultant's duty has been discharged. The consulting neurologist was thereby "covered" and presumably made immune to
any criticism that might be forthcoming later. The important
thing is what's been entered into the chart, not the patient, and
so this kind of doctor brings off the phenomenon of the tidy,
appropriately recorded, medical mess. In this instance the mess
was her failure to see to it personally that an infant with a
dilated pupil got emergency treatment quickly enough to relieve the elevated intracranial pressure and was sent to x-ray
for the CAT scan. It could be said she wasn't really much of a

treating doctor at all. She would be better likened to a medical pencil pusher or a medical officer prone to do nothing but stand around and give orders. However, the troops, the younger doctors, were off somewhere and presumably on other errands or just out of touch at this particular moment. Those younger doctors, very good at scribbling their off-the-mark confidences into the hospital chart, did not get to rewrite the neurologist's recommendations as orders to be followed by the nursing staff for another three hours.

And so this neurologist simply departed, having also penned her diagnosis of bacterial meningitis complicated by a possible "subdural effusion." It would certainly have been better if her insights had led her to personally direct a mannitol infusion as well as a timely removal of the infant to x-ray for a CAT scan. It would also have been better for her to tarry through the performance of the CAT scan, and hopefully, to engage a neurosurgeon personally summoned by her, in discussions of further management based upon the CAT scan findings. Hard to conceive that this neurological overseer was off to some more important emergency than that of tending the needs of this desperately sick infant. Hours later, an intern just happening to spot her recommendations, rewrote them as orders.

The neurosurgeon was one year out of residency training. He looked at the CAT scan and also read the neurologist's diagnosis of a possible subdural fluid collection. He considered that the type of fluid accumulation predicted by the neurologist might very well be either the clear kind of "serous" effusion commonly encountered in cases of bacterial meningitis or, more dangerously, one consisting of pus, a so called "empyema" of the subdural space. In either event it had to be removed, not only to relieve the pressure, but if the collection turned out to be pus, its evacuation would enhance treatment of the infection.

Hard to tell what gave him his mind set. The only thing demonstrated in the CAT scan was a swollen brain, and the swelling affected primarily the left side. There wasn't any subdural effusion. The diagnosis of the neurologist should certainly not have influenced him. After all, hers had only been a presumptive diagnosis, considered before the CAT scan was performed. She hadn't even had an opportunity to see the CAT scan. She was gone before it was carried out, and if ever there was a CAT scan that excluded the presence of any kind of subdural collection, this was the one. The surface of the swollen brain could actually be seen to press up against the skull. There was no subdural space at all, much less room for one to collect anything. Whatever this neurosurgeon might have learned in training, it wasn't what was needed for him to be competent in the interpretation of CAT scans. Unfortunately, a neurosurgeon who can't read x-rays is not equipped to do neurosurgery, and has no business attempting to do so. Without such skill it is hard to decide where, when, or even whether or not to operate. This doctor would also prove lacking in the competence required for assumption of the medical, the non-surgical aspects of the care he now found himself charged with.

According to his note, he did recognize from the scan that the infant's brain had shifted from left to right. He knew, also, that he had been summoned because one pupil had become dilated. How possibly could it then happen, aware as he was of the fact that mannitol, though ordered, was still not given, he wouldn't see to its administration?

What happened next was that the neurosurgeon decided to prove that the subdural collection which had not been demonstrated, and which did not exist, was in fact there, and to drain it. To that end he penetrated the cranial cavity with a needle, inserting it through a suture line of the skull near the outer margin of the infant's fontanelle. Only a few drops of normal clear fluid could be obtained. If the large collection still suspected by him had actually been there he should have been able to drain off a great quantity of fluid. It would have fairly gushed out. Having now demonstrated what any reasonable neurosurgeon would take for proof that there was no subdural collection, he took the infant to surgery, anyway, in order to operate for its complete removal. And still no mannitol.

He drilled through the skull, exposed and incised the dural membrane covering the brain. No fluid. Just the swollen brain as shown in the CAT scan. Under enormous pressure it burst through the opening he had provided and extruded, to stream like paste from a tube, becoming destroyed in the process. Peculiarly, he did not stop. He was undeterred, a man driven. Twice more he drilled holes in other locations, with the same result. It is impossible to abide these actions, like so many other medical or surgical maneuvers one may come across that make no sense. The inclination is so strong to keep searching for a reasonable explanation, some clarifying elusive justification which just isn't there.

All that was accomplished in the operating room was the infliction of great damage upon the left side of Eliani's brain. Now, if any bacteria were still present in the spinal fluid, they could directly invade the brain where the neurosurgeon had torn it, thus removing the natural barrier ordinarily preventing such bacterial penetration. In brain tissue damaged this way, the bacteria would find it easier to multiply. Although the brain was swelling even more, the infant, amazingly, was still alive. And as before, no mannitol.

No mannitol until twelve hours after surgery when the infant stiffened out with both pupils dilated and stopped breathing. Curious how that babe, when intubated and finally receiving the right medication, did with such vigor gulp life back into her throat and into what remained of her brain. It happened. It happened even though all of these inadequate doctors, continued to fail her and on at least three occasions gave her too little oxygen. It happened, even though when intracranial pressure surged once more from transient enlargement of the ventricles, hydrocephalus, they neither treated nor monitored her for that condition. Another enigma, that they never bothered about the hydrocephalus, and yet it was diagnosed by all of them.

How differently this infant, now a child, should have fared! There is no reasonable excuse for her need to limp through life with a spastic right arm and leg, retarded, comprehending little, dependent forever upon others, hardly able to express her needs or her pains. That's for sure. The infection, after all, was easily brought under control. The invading bacteria of the spinal fluid yielded readily to the very ordinary antibiotic medications she finally received. If only she had been treated promptly, in just that limited way, even at home she would have been better off. But she was in a major teaching hospital and tough as this infant was, she was no match for the doctors who treated her there.

This happened years ago near Boston. If one of the doctors presently concerned with Eliani's care were to need a copy of that hospital record, it could be reproduced for examination. It is 320 pages long, including 131 pages of progress notes written by physicians, as well as 18 pages devoted to consultative opinions. So much expounding! The very weight of all this documentation would probably incline the average reviewer to assume that an exhaustive, appropriate, and dedicated effort had been made in the interest of this baby. Especially so because on the first page of the record, in the place ordinarily reserved for notation of complications of treatment, nothing was entered regarding the uncal herniation after the spinal tap, or of the brain extruding from the burr holes during the unnecessary operation, or even of the postoperative respiratory arrest. On brief review there would not be any easily detectable clues to arouse suspicion of how bad the treatment was. Of course, any knowledgeable doctor might at least wonder why an infant with pneumococcal meningitis should have stayed so long in the hospital, or have such a voluminous medical record. This particular bacterial infection has yielded readily to medical treatment for more than forty years. A patient like Eliani should have been on her way in a week to ten days time, tops. Even so, the uncovering of precisely what occurred would be unlikely. Whatever they may think or suspect, doctors have no inclination to speak critically of one another. They have an understanding. They may not second guess colleagues, or raise questions regarding the sacred cow of "clinical judgment."

But does any one really need to plow through that enormous hospital record or ponder the significance of each one of its many written entries in order to know for sure that many things went wrong? Would it not be enough to merely read that although mannitol was urgently recommended on at least two occasions, it was not given until much later? Or that a baby with meningitis, responding to treatment, wound up in the operating room with excessive blood levels of phenobarbital and her brain extruding from burr holes placed surgically in her skull? One could come by the knowledge of care gone awry just by a bare glance at the order sheets, the medication records, the preoperative lab reports, or the operative note dictated by the neurosurgeon.

An examination of this tragedy was facilitated by the niceties of the law. It is illegal to destroy hospital records. After a certain period of time they can only be disposed of if microfilmed for future availability. That requirement is made in the interest of patients and for the general welfare of society. Would that court records concerning claims that go to litigation in such instances were also preserved. They are destroyed unless the party ruled against adversely by jury or judge should choose to enter an appeal. Only then may they sometimes be partially preserved. And when cases are settled out of court, the details of those agreements are sealed and generally protected from public scrutiny unless the settlement amounts are very high. Doctors quick to settle out of court, the worst kind, may hardly leave any trail at all.

This neurosurgeon appeared solemn when he strode from the room in which he had finally agreed to a payment on his behalf as part of a general settlement agreement with the infant's mother. His attorney, a graying, ivy league type, mustachioed and pin-striped in a well-groomed Brahman fashion, advised him sternly and with staunchness to take heart, to put it all behind him. "You gave it your very best. That's all that anyone could reasonably have asked. No one can ever say you are not a fine man and a wonderful neurosurgeon."

Perhaps the doctor has changed that much. Back then, when he operated upon Eliani, he seems to have been quite a bungler.

10

Recurrent Musings

Symptoms require that physical examinations as well as other kinds of diagnostic evaluation be made to establish their cause. For much of clinical symptomatology it is possible to detect the relevant underlying medical abnormalities. A range of appropriate therapies is known to doctors for most diseases. If not, they can be sought after and identified by consulting the medical literature and nowadays, even the internet. There would seem to be an inevitable sequence: symptoms, findings, treatment. But these are not the actualities.

Symptoms may not be given the attention they are due. Physical signs can go undetected or be noted, but not heeded. Tests that produce graphic images of disease processes and pertinent laboratory data can fail to be performed, or are carried out but misinterpreted. Knowledge of the existence or the variety of suitable remedies is not uncommonly faulty. Consequently, the medical or surgical treatment that's required (and which is never more than a prospect), needing for its realization a reliable, operative interface between the theoretical offerings of medical science and some person acting as health care provider, may fail to materialize. Known treatments and cures elude patients. At issue then becomes the reasonableness for continuing to assume that the human beings currently providing health care, and who are big on ingenuity and enterprise but, often enough, short on both reliability and dedication, should continue to be the primary providers of what, in order to be effective and consistent, must inevitably become a more automatic process.

It is certainly not science which has let patients down. Medical knowledge, in fact, has had steady, sometimes explosive, incremental growth. It is something else. Sick people, made all the more vulnerable by an encouraged dependency upon physicians for care and empathy, have not only been served poorly, but exploited through the privilege allowed doctors to exercise what can be an uninformed free hand but which is called "clinical judgment and discretion." Patients would do well to question the medical profession's leanings toward such vagaries, as well as its presumption of innocence under that guise when things go wrong.

In the address of catastrophic medical situations medical planners would do better to look to the prospect of help from sophisticated, near perfect, medical devices than to operate under the unrealistic assumption that doctors or their new money oriented managers will be the answer. Medical automation holds more promise for those who are sick than any kind of individuated personal response from a physician. After all, the possibilities of medical engineering are unlimited, while there is scant likelihood of altering the self-serving disposition of either doctors or the chief executive officers of the health maintenance organizations and managed-care insurance companies who now, in so many instances, control them. We know what it is to be human. As long as there is something lucrative or otherwise rewarding in it, the medical profession and its new overseers will not render reliable care to patients.

But how much longer can patients expect to have any voice in how they'll be treated when almost all of health care delivery has already fallen into the hands of business people and money managers seeking as their first order of business, no to render better care to patients but how to bleed as much money from the system by rendering less? If there are ample grounds for not trusting doctors with one's physical welfare, what is one to feel about a health care delivery system geared primarily for profit making and which for all practical purposes determines if, when, where, in what manner, and for how long those same doctors will treat people? Imagine a system which pays doctors a bonus on a regular basis for limiting the care they render but terminates their employment contracts if what they do, howsoever medically sound and indicated, is judged to be overly expensive. Imagine a system which controls what doctors may or may not advise their patients. Imagine a system wherein a clerk or a nurse decides whether or not a patient may or may not be hospitalized and for how long. Imagine new mothers getting no more than one night in the hospital and women having to have their mastectomies on an outpatient basis. Imagine a system wherein a life saving but very expensive drug is administered based entirely upon costs. Imagine a system which restricts the provision of care to the local community even though what is required is only available at a large medical center elsewhere, and that even in that local community patients must settle for the doctor assigned them although they do not like him and have good reason to suspect he is incompetent. Imagine, furthermore, that patients have no out because this is the kind of insurance plan their employer settled for. Why? Because it was the cheapest available. Only a few years ago, asked to imagine all of this, chances are a person would say: "What a nightmare! Thank God it can't happen here!" But it did happen. And for that, you can thank your doctors.

The situation has gotten so out of hand that on May 21, 1997 the Connecticut General Assembly passed legislation by a unanimous vote that lets the state overturn managed-care companies' decisions on what they will or will not pay for. It also bans "gag orders" preventing doctors from describing a range of therapeutic alternatives. President Clinton had previously appointed a commission to draft a "bill of rights" for managed-care customers so that they may appeal denials of coverage by their managed-care companies. But these actions stand to do no more than assure patients an external appeal process. First, they must appeal any denial of care to their insurance companies. No doubt about it. Even if the insurance companies are held to the requirement of a prompt response, with certain clinical conditions, by the time a patient gets an override order from the state he or she may be beyond help. Besides, patients who are very sick are not likely to have either the stamina or the resources to engage in this kind of a battle. It is another example of how easily the sick and the poor may be victimized.

Opinions expressed here relevant to the behavior of physicians need to be examined more closely. Irrespective of the fact that business people are now largely in control of how medicine is practiced, it is the personal conduct of doctors which has compromised health care as we have known it, not only by their occasional negligence or by their failure to stand up to the dollar oriented nonprofessionals now micromanaging the system in which most of them practice. The problem runs deeper than that.

It has been said that only five per cent of those employed in any endeavor are competent at what they do. This is not because of any lack of the potential for competence. It is because human beings subsist primarily for comfort or pleasure and in ways that avoid pain. And work? It is just the way to "earn a living." That phrase would seem to speak for itself, but the words, more often than not, are merely mouthed. Work, as ordinarily understood, is for earning the wherewithal to go on living. No more, no less. It is not to work well, but to work well enough to assure an existence. The pleasure of working well, or of excelling, is cultivated only by the few. In the modern world it is easy enough to work without ever thinking very much, even about what one is doing. Ninety-five percent of the population would appear to conduct itself that way. And the distractions provided by modern day opportunities to indulge in pleasure seeking are such that what will there is to work, or to work well, can be all too easily diverted from attention to the details of work. It is a misconception to assume that doctors, presumably entrusted with preservation of life, have different leanings, motivations, and concerns than any others with personal interests to be served. So how fare we as patients if only five percent of our physicians may be consistently competent, concerned about us, and enjoy doing what they do for its own sake?

It is natural and essential, of course, to aggressively seek advantage and pleasure, and to avoid pain. These are part and parcel of the behavioral endowment and evolutionary earnings of all successful species, and especially ours, with its impeccable ability to survive. The inherent advantage of being driven by self-interest is so essential to individual survival it came to be entrenched through genetic encoding. The further linkage of pleasure to forceful ways of implementing survival, however come by, fortuitous or designed, has turned out to be the fundamental trick for assuring survival. Of course, there is also in man a presumably encoded disposition for cooperative enterprise. The ability to maintain a satisfactory balance between what is important or pleasurable to the individual on the one hand, and the common interest on the other, is vital to group progress. But the operation of that balance is not a given. It only averages out. Progress stumbles in fits and starts, offset frequently by the consequences of individual self-seeking. So too, the medical scene presents a similar troubling vista. An endeavor presumed to be one of service and of "humanitarianism" is often self-indulgent, if not piratical, through no fault but our insistent genes. For this reason patients become, all too easily, a means to the personal ends and gratifications of physicians.

It is also true that the quality of medical care is at times influenced by both the instinctual and the acquired attitudes of physicians toward various personal attributes of patients. Treatment varies significantly because of that reaction of doctors to their patients. Doctors give better and more attention to the needs or demands of the affluent. Those who are physically attractive are also favored. Race and ethnicity influence the therapeutic formula. As in any encounter involving dissimilar biological types, behavioral stereotypes of wariness, aversion, or even overt hostility may be aroused. This happens more often than suspected. It is also unavoidable. It's in the genes.

Take the case of Willie. When he arrived in the emergency room with torn clothing, bruised, lacerated, exhaling a strongly fouled odor of whiskey, and also under the influence of cocaine, his neurosurgeon was put off by his appearance. The fact that he was head injured and having neck pain did not assure him the kind of care the doctor would ordinarily afford one of his more conventional patients. It took the doctor two whole days to determine that Willie had an obvious fracture dislocation of the cervical spine. Then, instead of stabilizing his broken neck in the accepted manner in order to promote healing and to prevent compression of the spinal cord, he did no more than order a follow up x-ray. That was the measure of his concern for a patient whose habit it was to urinate on the floor of his hospital room, and to ridicule nurses fetching Coca Cola when "coke" was what he really wanted. Willie was not a patient to be treated; he was one to get rid of. Because his second set of x-rays were taken with the neck in a position differing slightly from that in the original films, Willie's cervical vertebrae, at least at that moment, seemed to line up normally. Accordingly, he was discharged, although he still had a broken neck. No neurosurgeon should be so incompetent as to consider those x-rays to indicate anything but a dangerous and unstable fracture of the cervical spine. One moment his vertebrae were lined up right, the next, they weren't. Sooner or later, as they slid back and forth, they must at some point press upon his spinal cord and start to paralyze him. Such a trend had already begun, right there, even before his discharge.

By the time Willie was put out of the hospital, he could barely walk. One leg dragged behind him as he hopped along in a forward direction the while relying upon his girlfriend for support. She held him by the waist as he leaned upon her shoulder. If anyone had taken the brief time necessary to examine him, the signs of spinal cord compression were obvious and could have been spotted any time during the several days remaining before he was sent home in this outrageous way. Those were days during which his doctor avoided him. It would take a chiropractor to diagnose that Willie's neck was badly fractured and dislocated. Three days following his hospital discharge, in severe pain, weak by then in all four limbs, he was carried to this chiropractor's office. That gentleman needed but one x-ray to send Willie back into a hospital. It was a different one, however, because the first institution had the audacity to refuse him readmission. They had had quite enough of his kind. It mattered not that they had failed to diagnose his condition and were responsible for his paralysis. At all costs he was not to be returned to them. They didn't worry about liability. They just cared about not having to deal with patients like Willie. And the neurosurgeon who had discharged him from that hospital held Willie to be ungrateful, when a year later, he filed suit against him. After all, on the night he went out to see Willie in the emergency room, he wasn't even on call. "So much for being a good guy!" he said. And there was no hint of any sympathy for Willie's enduring pain, his flailing arm, or the weak legs he'd have to stumble along on for the rest of his life. It was not the doctor's disposition to be stirred by such a patient. It was not his pleasure?

What may be a doctor's pleasure? As it turned out for Willie, health care can come down to that. But it is a hankering which may have a fickle range, variable from day to day, and different among so many doctors. Also, the patient may fare well or poorly by the whim, the schedule, the rooted lifestyle, the prejudices and aspirations of a physician. One can board any commercial airliner with a greater sense of security.

1990. A study conducted at the Harvard Law School reports that in New York State during 1984, one out of every 25 patients was disabled by medical injury among 30,195 patients treated at 51 hospitals. One in four of these injuries was secondary to medical negligence. However, only one in eight of those patients who suffered from negligent care filed a suit, and no more than half of those who did take legal action received some form of compensation.

1991. President George Bush calls for a limit on the amounts of compensation to be paid to patients for pain and suffering due to medical negligence. This was one of his ways to build a kinder and gentler nation.

1993. President Clinton puts out the same call, as does Congress every year thereafter.

2001. Another President Bush follows his father's example.

Most politicians, it seems, can ill afford to cross the powerful doctor lobby. Patients turned victims draw no more sympathy from their representatives than when it was clear they needed better, more reliable, possibly universal health care but Congress does nothing about it.

Is it not inevitable that we turn to machines for better caring, diagnosis, and treatment? Things to come: periodic routine body scanning; blood and urine examination for certain kinds of definitive diagnosis; medical and non-invasive treatment automatically selected, quite specific and implemented under computerized control; human involvement only for innovation and to troubleshoot; medicine a matter of conceptual consensus and appropriate computer programming, rather than individuated professional discretion. This is the inescapable direction of health care until, by gene modification or therapy, the illnesses which plague us can be prevented from occurring. But we live in the present and must put into play, in line with certain obvious precautions, what resources we have.

Variety may be the spice of life, but uniformity, standardization, availability, reliability, are what promote its duration. Health care is not like automobiles, or fashion, or furniture, or entertainment. The ways in which we incline to amuse ourselves are irrelevant. There is no alternative but to provide the consistently best methods for managing an illness. It should not be acceptable that health care is different from hospital to hospital, or that one patient is treated differently than another. Not only is it not right, it cannot even be cost effective. However much standardization may be resisted for the exercise of special professional privilege or personal pleasure, it is clear that promotion of individual as well as group health, maybe even the welfare of our species, must involve adoption of such methodology. It has been a characteristic of other important advances. Sanitation, vaccination, water supply, counter measures to pollution and have been effective only to the extent they meet the requirement of availability and consistency. Perhaps a further indication of the need and the worth of standardization is its resistance by organized medicine. One need only recall how once that same profession objected to surgical instruments being boiled and sterilized to get a sense of its resistance to forward thinking. Years later, one could even encounter such behavior among those railing at the prospect of sick senior citizens being assured treatment under medicare! But, fortunately, there is a growing public resentment for the kinds of opposition to change that comes from vested medical interests, professional societies, and the sort of doctor who all too often sees patients only as a means to other ends. Their attempts to block progress increase that resentment and only foster a growing popular awareness that health care must be structured differently. Among the most vocal opponents of change one can sometimes spot those physicians especially apt to let their patients down. Only a few instances of their inadequacies have been described here.

Medical malpractice litigation of itself, contrary to how some would have it, will not force the adoption of medical standards, better patient care, or stricter supervision of physicians. It is not characteristic of human behavior to surrender special privilege, or to curb established, conditioned, appetites by simply coming under fire. But malpractice litigation is nevertheless a useful prod. It disquiets the public mind often affronting it profoundly as hidden tragedies surface and become spotlighted this way. Excitement over the innovative potential of a rapidly escalating medical technology should also impel progress. These two, together, may provide the provocative coupling needed for a more general insistence that changes be made.

Is it by some real stipulation that physicians have assumed the privilege of exercising broad latitudes of clinical judgment and discretion? It would appear that nowhere is it so written. Medical presumption, however, of there being such a self-serving stipulation provides doctors with broad leeway for much of their deviant professional behavior. In turn, what are all too often their overbearing pretensions, overblown claims, and outrightly arrogant attitudes have a way of influencing sick, vulnerable people to assume a childlike dependency, entrusting their health and their lives non-critically, unreservedly, to doctors whom they can no more than guess as being worthy of their confidence. For patients it is the comfort of surrender, of suspension of ordinary adult preoccupations and of release from the burden of exercising personal responsibility. Too easily they feel it opportune to revert to earlier, immature, ways. That behavioral pattern is always there to fall back on so why not do so, why not yield up their cares to another? And after all, doesn't the physician seem to know all that needs knowing, for their benefit?

But their doctor, concerned as he or she may be to master scientific detail, trades nevertheless on the profession's identification as an art, not a science, of healing. The relationship of doctors to their patients is affected profoundly by what is really a mystique. Thus the doctor becomes a veritable paternal or maternal guru. And after all, who could be expected to fully ascribe rhyme, reason, or rationale to what is an art, an "art of healing"? So doctors seldom explain symptoms, signs, or prospective or alternative treatment. They may omit necessary details of a patient's prognosis and discussions regarding whether there should be any treatment at all. Patients, all too willing to settle on blind trust, promote this kind of a relationship. The doctor has everything to gain from this unquestioning acquiescence to what he or she advises. There is a special comfort, also, for certain kinds of doctors who get to feel omnipotent in this unchallenged role playing. Even those not flawed by personal needs to be domineering can become intoxicated by such flattering subservience and behavioral regression on the part of their patients. Such doctors may develop not only an addiction for it, but also the conceit born of so much deferential regard. The inflated images seen by some physicians in their looking glasses may be distorted indeed!

To pursue this point further, in all fairness, by what valid argument can modern medicine claim to be an art, a healing kind of art, rather than a scientific discipline? Only as a science is it taught in medical school. Only science is pretended to in the medical literature. The main impediment to medical learning or skill is the difficulty in keeping up with a constantly expanding body of scientific technical information and know-how. It would seem that the only artful thing about the profession of medicine is its dodging of the responsibility to be appropriately straightforward and accurate in its dealings with sick people. The oft claimed insistence that medicine is just a healing art turns out to be little more than the defensively oriented, obfuscating, and standardly entered plea for immunity that doctors often respond with when they are rightly charged with medical or surgical inadequacy and hauled into court.

There is a modified disclaimer from my peers? Medicine, now admittedly, after all is said and done, is in fact a science, but simply not an exact one? Is this to be the revised pretense for shirking responsibility? But can anyone certify what is "exactly" so anywhere in this world, or elsewhere in the universe? And can eternal inexactitudes and recurrent confrontations with the limits of knowledge really be the basis for everlasting medical alibis, and not for what is not known, but for what should be, but is not? Your ordinary auto mechanic may plead many things in response to customer complaints for botching an engine overhaul, and after a few years of aging, the workings of an automobile engine can become mysterious indeed. But he would never insist on special dispensation as a practitioner of what is an inexact science! A mechanic would blush to even hint at what doctors are prepared to swear to!

Aside from the unavoidable handicap of their quite human frailties, physicians also labor under the charge of keeping abreast of a rapidly enlarging data base and other information. How effectively they treat patients bears directly upon their sustained and competent awareness of medical progress.

What alternative is there to some kind of automated revision of current methods of medical care when inevitably, the flow and the volume of new knowledge must come to exceed the capacity of even the more competent and dedicated of medical minds to comprehensively absorb it? Actually, that time is already upon us. And since the medical profession does not appear to exclude those with lesser intellectual and ethical endowment from its ranks, the matter of such reorganization becomes all the more urgent.

Increasingly, thereby, medical practice fails to benefit as it should from the proliferating technical resources available for its enhancement. But there is another kind of impediment to medical progress, based upon the fact that such progress is rarely prompted anymore by physicians themselves. Nowadays, a medical advance is apt to be the brainchild of industry and its own basic scientists, for whom physicians often serve as no more than hired point men. Medical innovation has been relocated from the university and the clinic to the pharmaceutical lab and the manufacturer's think tank. Doctors often provide no more than ceremonial trappings. They are the contact agents, the front running image makers of companies vying for position in a field shaped more than anything else by the need to stay competitive, a need which is also their only incentive for making progress. Even to identify those areas in which there exists a major clinical need for innovation, physicians are no longer the front ranked decision makers. But industry may not concern itself with clinical urgency, or the need to leapfrog long standing barriers to a healthier life. It may not focus its attention upon the most debilitating disease processes, such as cancer, but rather upon the surest avenues of access to the health care consumer dollar. Often, what is important to industry is the little upgrade, conferring some kind of inexpensive competitive edge, or the minor but significant enough advance in technology to make everyone else's expensive machine obsolete. According to the National Institute of Health Care Management Foundation's 2002 report, two-thirds of drugs approved between 1989 and 2000 were modified versions of existing drugs or identical to those already on the market. Industry, not doctors, lays out the priorities, and too often they are of that kind. Research and development can be oriented toward the quickest and most lucrative access to profit taking.

When doctors are recruited to conduct the clinical trials for various new drugs and devices that are new they may not even function as an adequate safeguard for the public. Industry has taken their measure. For the data concerning each patient studied, followed, and reported upon, they are often paid by the manufacturer of a new experimental product amounts of money commensurate or even exceeding what would ordinarily be earned by them through their alternative customary treatment of such patients. Since new treatments like this can only be licensed to a limited number of clinical investigators, these well paid doctors, working as clinical investigators, not only enjoy the benefit of a medical monopoly of sorts, they usually find that they are made busy by a swelling practice made up of patients who ordinarily would never have known of them, much less chosen to seek them out. No wonder they have such enthusiasm for certain new drugs and devices! Industry has their number in other ways. It is notable that physicians involved in early experimental trials have a way of being selected from the ranks of garden variety specialists, and not from the rosters of leading clinics or university hospitals out of which at least some modicum of critical or objective evaluation might be expected. Thus drugs and devices of very questionable effectiveness and safety go to market. The Food and Drug Administration does get to examine the data, but amazingly, it has no resources for making any kind of independent assessment! By the time such products eventually become available, many of them of questionable value and soon trailed after by all sorts of conflicting claims and reports of their relative merits and limitations, it is no wonder that doctors often play no more than a hunch when deciding upon whether or not to use them. And like any other kind of consumer, they are also highly apt to go for the manufacturing logo with which they have come to feel the most comfortable. Sales people of the drug industry, the "detail" men and women, have always been sent forth, at considerable company expense, to promote that kind of loyalty.

But no sooner does a physician begin to feel comfortable with a particular group of drugs or devices than he or she is barraged by new reports of further dubious but potentially profitable improvements made upon them. Medical industrial science is neither steady nor channeled for the general welfare. If it is anything, it is overly expensive, erratically directed chaos.

At the present time the average medical mind simply lacks the capacity to absorb the amount of information inundating it. Barely twenty thousand years ago, this same human mind put itself to rest on cave floors. It has probably not evolved much since then. How can it possibly be expected, now and in the future, to accommodate the expanding amounts of both genuine and spurious clinical data, as well as the byproducts of machines capable of sorting out atoms, molecules, energies, cells, tissues, stars, galaxies? Even with the computer as helpmate it is scarcely possible. Nor does diversification of approach or specialization of medical disciplines provide any alternative to the pressing need for automation of what is now a barely predictable human endeavor. Medicine, trying to cope with its exploding complexity, has already "specialized" and then "subspecialized." CAT and magnetic scanning, transplant medicine, gene splitting, the study of infectious disease, chemotherapy, internal imaging, PET scanning, genetics, are all new methodologies evolved as a response to particular clinical needs, yet destined by their shifting emphasis and expansion to spawn still other disciplines of research and therapy. But very little of this subspecialization has anything at all to do with the yeomen of medicine, passed over by this fragmentation, practicing on the mundane level of symptoms and clinical findings, and for whom a growing amount of this knowledge is not only unapproachable but more importantly, incomprehensible. Medical utopia should beckon from a closer and closer position, day by day, with each advance, but the ordinary doctor, its intermediary, is so outpaced by medical progress and confused by its complexity that he or she is transfixed as dumbly in its presence as was the Neanderthal in awe of the night star. Meanwhile, certain patients, because no one is really knowledgeably and competently in charge of their care, are behooved to stumble about from specialist door to specialist door, not really knowing which in particular to knock upon. Getting partial answers or no answers at all, their quest for proper treatment may go unfulfilled.

A doctor's brain is no different from any other. Each hour of every day, more of the cells which form it die and disappear. They cannot be replaced. They do not regenerate. Millions of them go that way. Less and less can be learned, remembered, retrieved, correlated. The capacity for patience, competence, diligence, even decency, also decline. How can that brain stand up consistently, ably, to the requirement of making appropriate disposition of the mounting information available to it? It doesn't. It can't. The possibility of confusion exists even in advance of the brain's eventual physical decline because overload always stalks it. Overload is predictable as new data rains down ever more oppressively upon the medicine man's brow, a brow which may also be eventually brutalized by nervous system disorders common to the aging process. Older men were once the wiser ones only because they had come to know more than they had forgotten and simple reasoning based upon experience could get them by. But those were simpler times which did not require them to learn very much. Times have changed and we require other, better resources.

Only a machine can be upgraded to protect it from information overload. Only a machine can be set to retain everything, and to do it consistently. Only a machine can be programmed to pace informational progression, and to make proper disposition of it. It has none of our limitations. Also, it alone can cope with its progeny. And what better deserves entrustment with the ultimate levels of human faith? Do we not already do so in the exploration of space? Sooner or later we must run out of patience with those human errors and blunders which cause the worst and the greatest number of our tragedies. And more of them are medical in nature than occur on railroads, highways, bridges and the runways of airports. Knowing where human well-being rests, our confidence is not apt to be in other people, but in the promise of better and better, ultimately flawless, machines. Nor shall we seek any longer after some other person as the surrogate for a long gone caring parent. Better to surrender our concerns and fate to the near perfect deliberations and calculations of devices lacking motivation. And if, somehow, we still require our medical deliverance to be rendered in a moral or ethical way, assuredly, machines are more apt to be reliably programmed to that sort of thing than is your average medical student.

Predictions: Genetic engineering will exclude many diseases now being confronted unavailingly at great expenditure of money and time. Medicine will be preoccupied with newly identified aberrations. Disease detection will be by periodic scanning at biomedical "convenience" centers, automated, cheap, universally available and financed by tax money. We owe ourselves that kind of physical security as much as any other. Why should there be a distinction between threats that are internal from those without? Machines will also identify whatever treatment may be indicated. Medication as needed will be dispensed on the spot. Treatment, more likely than not, will be curative, not just ameliorative. Requirements for more complicated kinds of management will be met at higher level centers. Very little hospitalization will be necessary. People will no longer be incised, laid open. It will be hard to imagine the fumbling surgical barbarism of past times. Smart molecules, designer antibodies, will make it obsolete. The days are long gone when medicine was a matter of "judgment," and much of it guesswork at best, or outrightly bad. For nominal cost and by universal coverage people will insert pass cards into machines and have it all. That providence approaches. It is not heralded by spoken predictions but by the mute presence of new machines crowding into strategic positions to care for us. Genetic replicators, imagers, endoscopes, analyzers, computers, high energy emitters, slave robots, not aping but rather finessing our medical methods and ambitions, readying themselves to promote a species. Overblown stuff? Look over your shoulder.

But until then, what does an ailing person do? One needs to be practical of course, but above all, vigilant. Patients must insist upon full explanations of their symptoms and the remedies proposed for them. If the doctor is not of a mind to give lengthy explanations, he or she is not the right kind of a doctor. One must not abide medical presumptions or professional condescension, or submit to blind faith accommodations rather than receive communications that are easily understood. In the event of uncertainty there should be no hesitancy about requesting second, even third, opinions. If a doctor says "it" will take time, what is "it"? What is being awaited? One should run from any doctor who treats adults as if they were children. And at least try to avoid doctors who are much too busy. Doctors in out-of-the-way places are not a good bet, particularly if much seems at stake. Do not accept diagnoses that are unsupported by laboratory data or radiographic findings. Critical care must only be sought from qualified physicians associated with major medical institutions and who have a verifiable track record. Look for hospitals and clinics having the most and the latest equipment. Avoid, especially in large teaching institutions, being anything but the doctor's "private" patient. If at all possible, steer clear of restrictive managed care. The reasons have been set forth. And be suspicious. Expect, in spite of the exercise of these precautions, that the care you receive may fall far short of what it might be from these same doctors, in these same places, but under different circumstances. A patient, for the time being, can not hope to be any more than an enterprising but prudent medical shopper. Whatever physicians may contrarily pretend, the patient, unfortunately, has never been anything but a relatively naive consumer in a service-oriented medical marketplace. The patient buys professional time, acquired skills, space, the services of expensive machines, medication. Empathy and professional morality, however desirable, have been neither marketed nor much available.

There are many different penalties, inconveniences, and losses to which uninformed shoppers are exposed in other kinds of profit-taking, service-oriented, transactions. The ones hazarded by patients while they search about for health care are unique and may be catastrophic. Better to be wide-eyed alert to one's risks than to fall victim in any way, including that of the grim kind of pupillary dilatation described in these pages. Any personal health care program that works, to whatever degree it may, is worth striving for.

Life, for some, may be only a worthless miracle, but still, it's all there is to cling to.

11

A Profession Without Standards

Not the medical experience anyone would choose, that's for sure. A land of patients left to their own devices, uncertain, confused, fumbling about for their best treatment options, offered few guidelines if any, and often not understanding those they do have. Medical automation is in its developmental phases but still no more than a vague prospect. Runaway doctors, under no real constraints, are held to no strict accounting either for the way they practice or for acts of medical negligence. So many problems have to be faced and others lurk that are faceless. Result? Too many medical and surgical tragic consequences.

It is easy to allege that an all too human self-indulgence on the part of physicians is to blame for this sorry spectacle. But is it possible there is some peculiarity in the way the medical profession conducts itself that facilitates its self-serving unaccountability and that this peculiarity can be remedied? It is odd that no one seems to pose this critical question. Nor does anyone even suggest ways out of the problem that begin to beg this question. How so when that peculiarity is fairly obvious? It is simply that the practice of medicine, by and large, is not held to stated, generally accepted, standards.

Is it not astonishing that the very subject of medical or surgical standards becomes only addressed during malpractice litigation when medical experts are testifying on behalf of plaintiffs or defendants, or when patients claiming compensation argue that they do exist and have been violated? In point of fact, very few coherent medical standards have ever been proposed. The American Board of Anesthesiology has insisted upon a few standards regarding certain minimum requirements for the monitoring of patients during anaesthesia and for the certification of those persons deemed qualified to administer anaesthesia. There are codified requirements relating to x-ray equipment, radiation exposure, and the handling of radioactive materials; and the Joint Commission for Accreditation of Hospitals places certain limited obligations upon hospitals for their administration, their laboratory functions, and record keeping. But for the innumerable medical and surgical conditions and practices for which specific standards of care could be easily set, none have ever been suggested, anywhere. All one ever reads about are the vagaries of "practice parameters" and "guidelines."

For years the American Medical Association has been publishing what it calls *A Directory of Practice Parameters*. On inspection it turns out to be little more than a spare compendium, a randomly selected listing of articles culled from the medical literature and sponsored by various medical organizations which recommend or critique or disavow various kinds of treatment, diagnostic guidelines, or monitoring methods for a confusing potpourri of illnesses. A doctor is free to either order a reprint of some particular article or entirely ignore the whole thing. It hardly matters which he does. In no article will he find himself held to any treatment standard. By putting out its "Directory" the American Medical Association has done no more than try to put a good face on a transparently bald bid for favorable publicity. It would be hard to imagine any kind of a good spin on this feeble effort.

In my own field of neurosurgery, although every imaginable treatment is eventually described in the scientific literature of medical journals and textbooks, what might be regarded as at least a minimum standard for the treatment of any condition has never been stated in so many words. For example, nowhere can anything be found to stipulate that "A patient rendered temporarily unconscious secondary to head injury must be kept in the hospital for observation. The standard of care requires it." Or, "The standard of care is such that a patient showing sudden dilation of a pupil is to be considered to have increased intracranial pressure and should be treated accordingly, as an emergency, until or unless that condition is excluded." Or, "A deteriorating but still reactive patient with CAT scan evidence of an intracerebral blood clot causing a five millimeter or more shift of midline brain structures requires emergency surgery." There is no reasonable basis for doubt that many of the patients described here would have been helped or even saved had such standards been stipulated and adhered to, particularly if considerable penalties were to be applied if they were not. The only place one might find such stipulations is in the chapter headings of the book you are now reading. Is it not reasonable to expect, given a particular diagnosis, that a physician would be required to use certain specific tests or certain treatment methods, and if not, he or she would have to contend with some kind of review process or licensing board? What does the privilege of medical licensure really mean if those who enjoy and profit from it cannot be effectively held to account for compliance, at the very least, with certain identifiable, well-known, minimum standards? If persons holding a driving license can be penalized for exceeding the speed limit, or sent to prison for hurting someone while driving under the influence of alcohol, then why should not physicians be subject to a disciplinary proceeding for failing to protect a patient's life or welfare when they fail to do what is incontestably called for, and it is supposed to be known to them? To plead ignorance could not be the way out. To do so would be to disqualify oneself for the treatment of that particular condition.

It would appear that doctors, even if they are complained about, only wind up being called to account for failure to conform to what are no better than medical vagaries, and never, accepted medical standards. And if the litigation of one of these complaints does finally attract medical as well as public notice, it does so only because of the large awards occasionally made to injured patients by juries. It is not because something in medicine has been vividly demonstrated and acknowledged to need fixing. It is also, in general, no matter of serious consequence if the doctors in question, on some rare occasion, may afterward face professional peer review. Typically, it is a quite tempered exonerating process utterly out of keeping with what may have just been decided in court. And in court it is forever the problem that instead of there being specific standards to which the doctor can be held accountable, he can only be held to the obligation of providing that level of medicine as it may happen to be practiced by the average prudent physician under "like or similar circumstances in the same or similar locality." What this may or may not amount to becomes a subject for days and days of courtroom testimony from a line-up of experts speaking to both sides of a rather esoteric argument. And well it might be an argument, one seemingly incapable of resolution, because everybody spouts a different opinion, even at times the doctors on the same side! Unfortunately for the injured party, the plaintiff, the greater credibility usually goes to the doctor's expert witnesses, often his local colleagues. After all, who should know better than the doctors who also practice medicine in that very community, commonly in the same hospital, what that standard might be? Of course, and it hardly needs asking, if these men are all cronies, even referring patients back and forth to one another, how objective can they be? Or if there is a locally endemic level of professional incompetence and all of these doctors in a particular setting are behind the times, then is it right that by the only law which presently applies, certain kinds of medical or surgical mayhem can be certifiably O.K.? No fault is to be found with the doctor? As things prevail now, the requirement of the only standard operating has been met. But it's a legal one! There's no medical counterpart. Some standard! Some kind of law!

But let some neurosurgeon, even one who is a professor, testify against a colleague, and he's apt to be called up by that same kind of peer review committee bent on excusing negligent doctors— except that in his case it will usually have embarrassingly painful consequences. An example? One man I know had the audacity to swear in court that it was inexcusable for someone to operate on the wrong side of the head and thereby to unnecessarily paralyze a patient! The neurosurgeon who gave that testimony received a six month suspension from his society and a reprimand. The man who operated on the wrong side of the head heard nothing more about it.

Would it be feasible to set real standards for a wide range of medical and surgical conditions? Yes. There are even examples to show it is not difficult to do so. Each year, under the auspices of the National Institutes of Health, free and open-to-the-public interdisciplinary meetings of health care professionals are held for "consensus-building" conferences regarding specific clinical conditions. Over a two or three day period agreements are reached as to those measures deemed necessary for establishing accurate diagnosis, as well as a range of acceptable kinds of treatment. In 1990, for neurosurgery, the subject was surgery for epilepsy. In 1991, it was treatment of tumors of the acoustic nerve. Subsequently there were others. If consensus can be reached that quickly by those who are knowledgeable about the current state of information as applied to a single disease process just happening to be selected for review, then certainly an in-depth and widened implementation of the same methodology could establish principles of diagnosis and treatment, expressed as minimum governing standards, for other conditions as well. Unfortunately, such conferees are not privileged to go so far as to suggest that their conclusions are to be construed as binding treatment standards. That is true, even though the conference summations insist that only certain specific therapeutic and diagnostic methods are deemed to be appropriate. No one seems inclined to declare actual standards. The need for certain methods of treatment, and the need of patients to have them, are apparently not to be set in stone for fear that down the road heedless physicians may be held to account for ignoring them. The latitude of doctors to use their own discretion, however faulty, must be preserved at all costs, costs often borne by damaged patients. For that reason, not only is the treatment advocated by these conferences usually ignored, but doctors don't even have to know about it, much less implement it.

That does not mean, however, that such an approach, if taken to a logical and insistent end, would not meet the objectives required for the betterment of society. Nor does it detract one bit from the obvious fact that it would be relatively easy to reach a quick "consensus" for various standards of treatment, once doctors have accepted rationale for it.

There are still other ways to accomplish this same end. Physicians, particularly medical specialists, who want to be certified as competent and as being under obligation to keep abreast of medical advances in their chosen fields, must submit themselves, after training, for examination by an appropriate "American Board." If they pass examination, they can trade on the result of that certification. They can use it to establish themselves in their communities as credible, qualified, practitioners, eligible for various hospital appointments and the award of operating privileges. Although those examinations seek to test the level of their scientific knowledge, they may not determine whether these doctors know how to act in a wide variety of clinical circumstances. Even where examining boards, under the influence of the American Medical Association, require subsequent recertification to see if doctors have actually kept up with medical progress, again, the examinations are more apt to deal with data in the abstract sense, and not with the implementation of it for purposes of treatment, in compliance with some acknowledged treatment standard. A doctor, his or her head filled with an enormous amount of abstract clinical and scientific irrelevancy, may pass with flying colors, and yet have no understanding of how he or she must act in some particular emergency or other circumstance. The certifying boards have completely ignored any sense of responsibility for meeting the obligation to prevent this. The boards have all of the necessary resources to do more than they do. And after all, they foist these doctors upon the public as certified specialists. So why can't they also set minimum standards of care and require that their diplomates meet them? This should not be either a difficult or inordinately time consuming task. The NIH consensus building conferences manage to do it nonbindingly and there aren't that many conditions needing to be addressed.

And if the profession will not, through its own agencies, accept such responsibility in line with its stated principles of ethical conduct and its public oath taking, then it is time for governmental intervention. The government has the funds, and the potential capability; it should also have the motivation to set standards for medicine no less than it does for other activities standing to compromise the public safety. It is not an acceptable argument that governmental regulation of foods or drugs or transportation is often poorly administered and enforced. The failure to implement standards can always be remedied. But without stated standards, there is no deterrent for irresponsible or ignorant action, and no foundation, either, for improvement.

Let it be understood that what is being advanced here is not a case for cookbook kinds of medicine. Medicine is too complicated and too much in evolution to be administered that way. But there are always, for every illness, some generally agreed upon minimum principles of contemporary treatment that are identifiable and important enough to deserve advocacy as standards of treatment. As time passes, and medical progress is made, they may be correspondingly abandoned, changed or upgraded.

At present, for example, medical knowledge should dictate that a patient suffering the effects of acute spinal cord injury receive certain kind of treatment within a few hours following injury. An emergency room physician not knowing that, and failing to do so, should be held accountable for the consequences of his inadequacy. Looking back on the other cases described here, it was counter to prevailing knowledge, and should have been regarded as a violation of standard, for the two patients with vascular malformations of the brain to have been operated upon in the absence of any evidence that they had ever suffered from intracranial bleeding. The ordinary indications for such surgery, stated as a standard, would not include any condition existing for either one of them at the time they were operated upon. If an appropriate standard had been in place, a neurosurgeon choosing still to operate upon such a patient would only do so at the risk of suffering the consequences of his or her deviation. The physicians treating the baby Eliani for meningitis should have been under the mandatory requirement of doing a spinal tap and instituting antibiotics immediately. They should not have delayed it for more than two hours. And the neurosurgeon who operated upon the same infant should have been under the obligation of desisting from an operation for which he had no indication, because both the CAT scan and the subdural tap he had performed were negative. It is as simple as that and it is possible to go on and on.

How should violations of medical standards be managed? Methods of surveillance for their detection would have to be worked out. It would not be difficult to devise ways that hospital administrators and accrediting commissions could implement. Then there would also have to be developed a range of penalties for infractions, running from reprimand to variable suspension of specific hospital privileges, requirements for retraining, or even loss of medical licensure. It is also reasonable to consider that certain kinds of malpractice, which border upon the egregious and lead to extreme injuries of patients or death, should be looked upon as offenses of a criminal nature and be adjudicated accordingly. This has already happened. Hopefully, certain kinds of doctors, those not particularly inclined to conscientious or high minded endeavor, when faced with mandatory penalties for specific violations of clearly stated medical standards, would hold themselves to levels of performance not to be obtained from them by alternative measures.

It needs also to be considered that straightforward statements of medical standards, and imposition of penalties for their violation, would probably go a long way towards eliminating most malpractice litigation. Such activity is about nothing so much as it is about protracted arguments and legal maneuvering over what the standard of care may or not be in any instance. State them clearly, once and for all, and there would be nothing left to argue about. Who would want to defend against a claim having unchallengeable merit, or plead a claim obviously devoid of it? Establishment of definitive standards is a clear way out of the enormous costs, the loss of time, and the grief entailed in all such litigation. The public, as well as doctors faced with escalating malpractice insurance premiums and non- meritorious claims, have much to gain from that kind of innovation.

Contrast such an approach to that advocated by David Palmisano, the President-elect of the American Medical Association. This physician spokesman wrote that "although the physician may aspire to give the best care, the law does not require the best. The law requires a minimally acceptable level of care, thus my analogy to the 'low hurdle.'"

So doctors are not to give patients their very best. Rather they should give as little as they can get away with. The little bit they presume the law allows.

Substandard medical and surgical treatment does not always bring a patient to grief. In fact it commonly fails to produce symptomatic or detectable injury. But although it may not cause a patient physical or emotional pain to have her uterus removed for no good reason, merely because it is done skillfully enough, it is no less wrong. It should not be considered any less an affront to the patient, or any more an experience patients should have to endure or doctors be financially rewarded for. Society can well do without the burden of these kinds of malpractice, only lesser because they are better tolerated. The kinds of doctor committing them, however, are a financial drain on society and stand also to eventually cause serious injury. Such practices are apt to decrease under the pressure of enunciated standards carrying penalties for their violation. It also bears remembering that the greater number of patients injured by medical negligence never do seek satisfaction in court, often because they are unaware that such an event has taken place. They are accepting of too many complications called justifiable by physicians. They deserve to be compensated, however, and straightforward statements of what a medical standard was required of their physician would probably deliver many of them from their state of unsuspecting ignorance.

The adoption of bona fide medical standards would also address an urgent mounting health care dilemma. The fundamental problems inherent in so-called health maintenance or managed care insurance programs have already been commented upon. But there is still one other. Surreptitiously, without it ever being approved by physicians as medically valid or even humane, health care is being "managed" everywhere in this country in compliance with requirements that actually constitute ersatz standards. No one has ever passed any official or consensus kind of judgement upon them. And these illegitimate codes of professional conduct are not only arbitrarily formulated and imposed but represent a danger of potentially inestimable dimensions. Aside from the fact that they engender that selfsame human disposition in doctors we have the most cause to rue, these largely inappropriate and money driven codes of professional behavior have directly injured patients and are oriented toward seeing sick people only as a means to profit oriented financial ends. This situation came about because there was a void. Not only had the medical profession failed to ever set up appropriate standards for itself but when negotiations to establish universal single payer government or alternative private health insurance plans collapsed in the face of partisan politics, the field was abandoned to mercenary forces patiently awaiting their moment. Also, the ground was ripe for just such a takeover because the government, uncaring about the fact that treatment is of people and not diseases, was putting into place a system which not only capped what would be paid to doctors and hospitals for the treatment of specific illnesses and procedures under Medicare but also cut about 65% from what it was willing to expend for the care of the indigent, shifting that expense to states, local governments, and private hospitals.

Most hard hit were those institutions we depend upon for innovation, research, teaching, and cutting edge methods of treatment—our medical schools with hospital affiliations. Brought to their financial knees in short order, such institutions have been veritably swallowed up into managed care organizations, for-profit hospital chains, awkward overreaching affiliations with one another, and even mergers into holding companies which totally control their purse strings. Hardly does it seem that anyone out there is caring much about the fact that in every way conceivable, for now and the future, sick people are going to have to make do with less and less while those running this horrendous system stand to get richer and richer. The system has to be reworked and the easiest and most logical way of bringing it about remains the same. All that is needed is to realize that managed care feeds on the innocent and the ignorant and turns a mighty profit by operating in a professional and moral vacuum. If responsible, forward thinking physicians were to regroup and formulate once and for all an array of standards requiring that both doctors and hospitals own up to their obligation to do the very best that can be done for their patients we would be where we need to be very quickly. We would be caring for the sick once more in nonprofit institutions and in ways that would make what is currently going on, impossible. You can not make heaps of money off of the backs of sick people unless you consistently exploit them. Proper medical care, expertly rendered and managed, is never more than a break-even proposition, often requiring private endowment and government support. If the venture oriented medical impresarios driving the system now were to be held to high and stringent standards, what could such speculators do but abandon the field? Would they relish the prospect of facing an enormous number of legally mounted charges of negligence under circumstances whereby their negligence, by virtue of accepted and adopted standards, could be easily proved?

What has been discussed here is not for notice as a matter of passing interest. It is intended as a means of raising questions of urgent public concern. People have been coping, struggling, or dealing unsuccessfully with the problem of medical negligence for a very long time, but only as individuals. For all of the occasional isolated instances of their success, their efforts have been unproductive of any material change in the way medicine is either practiced or monitored, except for the advent of superfluous, unnecessary, and expensive testing of patients which doctors have instituted under the misguided notion it can prevent them from being sued.

Medical practice has gone unrecognized as a seriously flawed human endeavor, requiring not our individual reproach but very careful regulation. This is all the more so now that the organizers of managed care have entered the field, arranging not for better care but the institutionalization and promotion of those selfsame flaws. The remedy for this dilemma is there to be seen. There is a need to control the practice of medicine by invoking standards for professional conduct and care, and it is self-evident. It requires only the kind of determined response to which people as a society usually resort when they are collectively threatened.

Adopted, those standards will be all we have to count on until something better comes along, something that gets us around the marvelous but mischievous human factor.